MORE STRANGE SCOTLAND

JACK'S STRANGE TALES BOOK 6

JACK STRANGE

Copyright (C) 2020 Jack Strange

Layout design and Copyright (C) 2020 by Next Chapter

Published 2020 by Reality Plus – A Next Chapter Imprint

Edited by Terry Hughes

Cover art by Cover Mint

All rights reserved. No part of this book may be reproduced or transmitted in any form or by any means, electronic or mechanical, including photocopying, recording, or by any information storage and retrieval system, without the author's permission.

For Cathy, the wife of a strange man.

ACKNOWLEDGMENTS

I would like to thank the following people for their help, guidance, knowledge and craic during my often-aimless wanderings around the strange little country of Scotland:

Graeme Ritchie for kick-starting this book, Archie Kilner of Peebles for his often gruff and always kindly anecdotes of Peeblesshire, that unknown man at the harbourside at Scrabster for his dry humour on a very wet day, and all the other nameless, humorous and patient people who have contributed to the contents of this book. Most of all, of course, I thank the wife-woman, just for being herself.

INTRODUCTION

A few years ago, I wrote *Strange Tales of Scotland*, a collection of stories that included folklore, history, ghosts, monsters, castles and various strange and, I hope, interesting anecdotes. Since the book's publication, some people have castigated the book as nonsense while others have asked for more of the same. Until recently, I managed to avoid the temptation, for I thought I had finished writing about strangeness, having added Wales, England and Ireland as well as the sea to my strange series. However, last year my wife-woman and I moved house from Moray in the north east of Scotland to Angus, in the old Pictish heartland. In this region, it is impossible to turn a corner without finding history or a strange happening.

For instance, within a two-mile radius of our present home, we have an old toll house, a Pictish fort, a haunted cottage (that we nearly bought), a reference to a temple I am unable to trace and a farmhouse named after an alleged cannibal. Add another few miles, and we have a battlefield where the Scots defeated the Norse, a castle that was heavily involved in the Rough Wooing and a fairy legend. When I spoke to a local tractor man, Graeme Ritchie (who also happens to be my son-in-law), born and bred in Angus, he told me a couple of local legends that were too good to ignore.

And so I thought I'd include them in another strange book. I will put the first of Graeme's stories here as a taster of the strangeness to come. At present, we live in a small village a few miles outside Dundee, surrounded by the fields of Angus. Behind our house, a path strikes north and east. It is an ancient path, which has probably been in use for hundreds if not thousands of years, connecting several cottages, an old smithy and a couple of farms. One of these farms has the name of Denfind, and herein lies the story.

In Scotland, a den is a small dip or a valley, often wooded, and not far from Denfind Farm there is such a place. The modern road passes this wooded valley, which to my strange mind, may well be the scene of the following events.

A few hundred years ago, travel within Scotland was difficult. The roads were rudimentary at best and often infested with bands of sorners – outlaws. For variety, add reivers in the Borders and caterans (Highland raiders) in the lands immediately south of the Highland line. To make matters worse, in this corner of Angus, north east of Dundee, travellers began to go missing. History is vague about the date, but probably some time in the 15th century.

According to the legend, a family lived in the wooded den just south of the village of Monikie, and they kidnapped travellers, murdered them and ate them. Not surprisingly, the area became notorious, so the name Fiends' Den or Den of the Fiends was coined for the cannibals' location. The cannibals seem to have been very similar to the better-known Sawney Bean's family, or perhaps were an echo of that notorious clan. The cannibal clan at the Fiends' Den were said to have a taste for tender meat, so preferred younger victims, but as fewer trav-

INTRODUCTION

ellers passed by, they began to raid the local villages, ferm-touns and cottages for children and young adults. The Angus people soon worked out what was happening and marched en masse to the Fiends' Den to mete out summary justice.

The authorities, or perhaps just the local population, executed the entire cannibal family except for the youngest, a mere baby. The locals spared her as she could not yet have tasted human flesh. This child was adopted by parents who did not tell her from where she came. However, within a few years, the girl displayed alarming signs of having the family trait, attacking children and licking blood from open wounds. It seemed that the cannibal genes were also present in her.

Her adoptive family observed the young cannibal, giving her advice and as much help as they could but, as the girl grew into young womanhood, it became apparent that she also was a cannibal. When she was 18, the local authorities executed her at Dundee's Seagate, and her last words were said to be: "If ye had tasted human flesh, you would think it so delicious that ye would never forbear it again."

Today, only Fiends' Den or Denfind Farm recalls the legend, and possibly the name of the farm suggested the story. However, that gruesome little tale started me off on my investigations again, searching for anecdotes new and old to compile into another book about the strange myths, legends and possibly even facts in Scotland. Some I have previously published as stand-alone articles, others I found recently, and many people have told me tales over the years that I have stored away for future use. Here is the result and I hope you enjoy them!

Jack Strange

PART ONE
STRANGE PLACES

THE STRANGE ISLAND OF SKYE

THERE WAS no bridge the first time I travelled to Skye. It was a real island then, with a short ferry journey from the mainland and a thousand legends waiting in the glens and hills. From the ferry, I could not see much of the island; I could not see much at all, for a thick white mist covered everything, from the Cuillin Mountains down to the Kyle of Lochalsh.

I am not sure what I think about Skye. For those with the ability to feel the "power", as Bowed Davie of Peebleshire's Manor Valley called it, Skye has an indefinable *something* that lingers in the atmosphere. For others, it is merely an island of dramatic scenery or a place to settle to escape the rat race of the south. I find it an unsettling island, more disturbing than any other part of Scotland, as if the island is waiting to reclaim itself, and the hills and mountains were watching, brooding, aware that all is not as it should be.

To some, Skye is *Eilean a' Cheo*, the Island of Mist, yet that is a modern name, coined when misty scenery was deemed romantic. A reverend gentleman by the name of JA MacCulloch made the nickname famous in 1905 with the publication of his book *The Misty Isle of Skye*. There certainly is mist on Skye, as there is on any island with hills, but probably no more than average. What there is on Skye is a plethora of folklore, myth and legend.

Skye: Of Names and Castles

Every hill, every loch and village in Skye has its stories, with each often interlinked with others on the island. Take, for example, Beinn na Cailleach, a mountain that overlooks Broadford. The name means the Hill of the Old Woman, although nobody is sure which old woman it honours. One theory is that it refers to the strangely named Saucy Mary, who allegedly stretched a chain from Kyleakin in Skye across the Kyle of Lochalsh to the mainland, to make any ships pay a toll before they could proceed. In common with many Scottish hills, Beinn na Cailleach has a cairn on the summit.

More is known, or conjectured, about the 16th-century Castle (or Caisteal) Uisdean. This battered ruin sits beside Loch Snizort Beag, or Little Loch Snizort, just north of the Hinnisdal River mouth in Trotternish. Castle Uisdean means Hugh's Castle and the builder was said to be Hugh MacDonald of Sleat, a son of the 10th Lord of the Isles. Castle Uisdein would have had a single gate, reached by a ladder, which the occupants of the castle would haul inside for security. There is nothing picturesque about this square tower house, while its surroundings can be rather bleak in foul weather. However, there is a strange little story.

Hugh, or Uisdean MacGillespig Chleirich to give him his correct, Gaelic, name, had a notion of becoming chief of the clan. Hugh was not a man one would care to have as a neighbour. Indeed, a song of the time asked why his foster-nurse did not crush him to death when he was a child, to prevent him from growing into such an unpleasant adult.

At that time, the chief was Donald Gorm Mor, Sir Donald MacDonald of Sleat. The fact that Donald was Hugh's uncle seemed not to concern Hugh, who planned a neat little murder. Hugh's idea was to invite Donald Gorm to Castle Uisdean and have a few handy lads around to thrust a dirk through his ribs, direct and straightforward. To that end, Hugh wrote a couple of invitations; one to Donald Gorm, asking him to come to the castle, and another to the intended assassin, giving details of the plan. However, the letters crossed in the post, and Donald Gorm was very interested in reading all about his forthcoming murder. He asked his followers to bring Hugh to him to discuss the matter in person.

Not surprisingly, Hugh fled Skye and holed out at Dun an Sticir on North Uist in the Outer Hebrides. The name means Fort of the Skulker and it is a 16th-century building on an Iron Age broch, ruined now but still worth a visit. However, Donald Gorm sent out search parties and, in 1601, Donald's warriors hauled Hugh back to Skye. Donald Gorm ordered him to be interred in a dungeon at Duntulm Castle, with a hunk of salted beef to eat, and a pewter water jug. Hugh ate the salt meat but when he went to drink the water, he realised the water jug was empty. And then the stonemasons began to seal the dungeon door, leaving him to a lonely, agonising death by thirst. According to the legend, Hugh went mad inside his terrible dungeon.

It was decades before the wall was broken down during alterations to the castle and Hugh's skeleton was discovered. He was said to have chewed on the empty pewter jug before he died. Another story claims that Hugh's skull and thigh bones decorated the window of the church at Bornaskitaig until as late as 1827.

Donald Gorm was not the most pleasant of men, either. According to another legend, he married a sister of Rory Mor MacLeod, the MacLeod chief who lived at Dunvegan Castle. Donald's wife was a good woman but unfortunately had only one eye. When Donald Gorm took a fancy to another woman, one of the daughters of Mackenzie of Kintail, on the mainland, his present wife had to go.

Finding a one-eyed horse, Donald thrust his one-eyed wife on top, scoured the island for a one-eyed boy to lead the horse and a one-eyed dog to follow, and sent the whole sorry procession to Dunvegan in a calculated insult. Naturally, Rory Mor retaliated, and the two clans began, or probably resumed, a feud that spread as far as the MacDonald lands of Uist and led to the deaths of men, the ravaging of women and burned homes. There was little romance in the old days of clan warfare.

Donald Gorm's Duntulm Castle stood powerfully on a promontory above the sea but is now a total ruin. According to legend, the MacDonalds of Sleat abandoned Duntulm in the 1730s when a nursemaid dropped the chief's son on to rocks below the castle. In revenge, Sleat thrust the nursemaid into a boat and left her in the Atlantic without oars or sails. The nursemaid's ghost, and that of Hugh, are said to haunt the ruins of the castle, both screaming. They are not alone, for Donald Gorm also remains, apparently spending his death in battling other, unknown spectres, while his one–eyed wife looks sorrowfully on. The legend of the nursemaid dropping a baby is not unique, for Findlater Castle on the Moray Firth has the same tale.

Despite Duntulm's stories and ghosts, of all the castles of Skye, Dunvegan is arguably the most famous. The ancestral home of MacLeod, it sits proudly beside a loch of the same name. It is a castle with a long history that includes comedy as well as tragedy. One episode occurred during the American Revolutionary War, when the owner, General MacLeod, was fighting in North America.

The Scottish-born United States seaman John Paul Jones was known to be prowling the seas off Scotland, pouncing on ships and raiding on shore, so Dunvegan's factor decided to remove any valuables from Dunvegan. He had hardly begun when *Bon Homme Richard*, Jones's ship, sailed boldly into Loch Dunvegan with her cannon manned and the flag of the newly proclaimed United States flying at her masthead.

For a moment it seemed that Jones was about to send his crew to ravage Dunvegan, until the sound of bagpipes floated across the loch. It is easy to imagine the tension, with the people in the ancient castle watching the modern warship creeping across the dark water. Her star-spangled flag would be challenging all comers and the black mouths of her cannon threatening the defiant civilians – and then the pipes wailed.

Every eye swivelled to the head of the loch, where a lone piper led a long procession of men that marched slowly towards the castle, two by two in formation. Guessing that Clan MacLeod had risen to repulse him, Jones decided that discretion was far better than valour, weighed anchor and sailed away as fast as his ship would take him. If he had waited another five minutes, he might have learned that there was nothing martial about the newcomers.

Donald MacLeod, the Swordale tacksman had died a few days earlier, and the piper was leading the funeral procession on its way to Kilmuir Graveyard.

Dunvegan, naturally, has older tales. There is a cave on Loch Dunvegan, near Borreraig, known as the Piper's Cave, that has at least two legends attached. The first is the common cave-story about a piper who entered playing his pipes and subsequently vanished. In this instance, the piper was one of the famous MacCrimmons, whose piping college was not far away. As so often, the piper entered with his dog, and the music of his pipes became fainter and fainter until the dog returned alone. According to legend, people can still hear the piper sometimes, trying to find his way home. One version of the legend says that MacCrimmon's piping enthralled the fairy queen, so she kept him enchanted underground, and that is how the famous pipe tune, *MacCrimmon's Lament,* was composed.

The second legend is more prosaic and possibly more accurate, as it claims that pipers used this cave for practice. The piper I asked, a lassie from Inverness, told me sourly that the pipe-major would probably order the young apprentices to the cave until they could produce something that sounded bearable.

There is another cave in Skye, the Uamh nan Oire, the Cave of Gold where another piper vanished. He was a MacArthur, one of the hereditary pipers of MacDonald. That story was current in the 17th century, although the actual cave, near Bornaskitaig Point, is disputed. The Isle of Barra also has its Uamh nan Oire, with a similar legend, except that predatory sea-dogs, of the four-footed variety, seized the piper. Hebridean caves were dangerous places for pipers.

Skye: Ghost Light of Broadford

Sometime in the late 19th or early 20th century, an Edinburgh doctor was on holiday at Broadford in Skye. In the evening, he walked by the shore and saw a bright light out in the bay. He watched it for a while, unsure what it might be, and then decided it must be a fisherman showing a flare.

However, the light did not behave as a flare should. It travelled slowly above the water, coming towards the doctor, and then it disappeared. In its place, a woman stood, huddled in a long cloak and holding a child in her arms.

Convinced he had seen a ghost, the doctor asked the innkeeper, who confirmed that a boat had gone down a few years earlier, and the sea cast the bodies of a woman and child on to the shore where the doctor saw them.

Skye: The Water Horse

In Uig, a dark lochan sits serenely beside a mountain pass. The locals knew that the lochan, although small, was also dangerous, and avoided its calm waters, telling each other tales of the strange creature that lurked beneath the waves. Like most lochs in Skye, there are many rocks at its side and, laddies being what they are, one herdsboy lingered to throw stones in the water. Why do children do this? To see how big a splash they can make, perhaps, or just because they can.

On this occasion, the herdsboy got ambitious, throwing in larger and larger stones until he began to roll in the huge boulders that lay beside the banks. Eventually, he realised that the water was vastly disturbed even when he had stopped throwing stones. Suddenly scared, the herdsboy hid behind a rock and watched as a beautiful black horse emerged from the lochan. The laddie gazed on as the water horse looked around it before returning to the depths, where it probably remains.

Knowing how dangerous water horses can be, it is unlikely that the boy threw any more stones into that lochan.

In common with other parts of the Highlands, Bracadale in Skye had its water horses, which were – or are – dangerous creatures to cross. They usually disguise themselves as beautiful horses that live in lochs and rivers while, in reality, they are monsters that kill and eat people. When a group of young women were at the shieling high on the Trotternish Ridge, a voice called from outside.

Speaking in Gaelic, the woman's voice asked to be allowed in, saying: "Let me in, you beloved children."

When the women opened the door, they saw an old woman standing outside. "Where will sleep the little old woman, tonight?" the old woman asked.

"At the feet of the maidens," the women said. The shieling had one communal bed, made of heather, on which all the women slept.

"Oh, the beast of the feet will take hold of me," the old woman said, looking frightened.

"You can sleep at the back of the bed if you wish," the kindly Skye women offered. Still, the elderly visitor was not happy, and only when the women said she could sleep in the centre of the bed was the visitor content. Soon the visitor and the Skye women were all in bed, with most sleeping. However, the Skye woman closest to the door was aware that the visitor was restless. The Skye woman looked around, to see the visitor had bitten a chunk out of another woman's arm.

"The water horse!" the woman yelled, and ran out of the door, with the visitor, now in its proper form as a water horse, in hot pursuit. On most days, a four-hooved water horse can catch a two-legged human, but fear added to the Skye woman's speed. She was still in front when she reached the burn that gurgled between Balgowan and Totarder, although the water horse was closing the gap.

As the woman leapt the stream, a cock welcomed the dawn in Balgowan. Like the Devil, the water horse cannot abide the crowing of a cock, and it shouted after its prey, "Duilich c, duillich c, alltan," which means: "Sad it is, sad it is, stream."

And that is how the Alltan Duilich, the Altan Streamlet, gained its name.

Skye: The Fairies

Naturally, in a place as uncanny as Skye, there was fairy lore. At one time a significant number of fairies lived in Skye – maybe they still do and are merely biding their time before they show themselves again. The people of Skye worked long hours at harvest-time, yet never laboured by moonlight. The moon was the fairies' lantern and it was bad luck to work then. Was that some ancient folk memory of moon worship?

At any rate, one married couple either forgot or scorned the old legend and were out one moonlit night, gathering their corn by sickle, the traditional method. They were engrossed in the harvesting until the husband felt a sudden sharp pain on his hand. He dropped his sickle, aware he had offended the People of Peace, and the couple returned home. In the morning they found an elf-shot, or fairy dart, on the ground. Elf shots were the ancient stone arrow-heads that people sometimes dig from the ground.

One of the most mystical fairy places is Fairy Bridge between Dunvegan and Waternish, for here three roads and three rivers meet. The number three is a significant number in many cultures, from West Africa to Scotland to the Middle East, so having a double three would undoubtedly give the Fairy Bridge an added advantage.

The bridge is a modern addition to the area, whose Gaelic name is Beul-Ath nan Tri Allt, or the Ford of the Three Burns, although another, more romantic Gaelic name is "a Ford for the Fairies".

The story predates the bridge by some centuries and refers to a time when the MacLeod chief wished to marry a local fairy girl. Such marriages were permitted to last only a year and a day, after which the fairy wife returned to Fairyland, or Elfhame, as we called it in Southern Scotland.

The couple parted at the Fairy Bridge, and the mother wrapped the son that had been born to them in a silk shawl. That shawl, known as the Fairy Flag, is still kept in Dunvegan Castle. The MacLeods can produce that flag to protect the clan in times of extreme trouble – but only three times. It has been flown twice, so the clan is saving the third time for some unspecified threat in the future.

Now, don't be thinking that the fairies of Skye are a gentle breed for, in the old days, Skye was renowned for its fighting fairies, who could be as violent as the human population. An example is what they did after the clan battle of Harta Corrie, beside remote Glen Sligachan. The fighting began at dawn and lasted until dusk and the bloodshed ended only when the MacDonalds had killed every warrior of Clan MacLeod. Elated after their victory, the MacDonalds dragged the MacLeod corpses to a massive rock now known as the Bloody Stone, which the hardy can see if they don't mind marching over rough terrain for miles. The Bloody Stone sits a mile or so north of Loch Coruisk. Anyway, for years after the battle, the Skye fairy folk visited the battle site to make arrows from the ribs of the dead MacLeods, which hardly seems like the action of a peace-loving people.

Other hill legends are less bloody, but still carry a bit of an edge. Take the Old Man of Storr, for instance. The Old Man of Storr is a rock formation, part of a ridge of hills that extends along the peninsula of Trotternish, the north-eastern wing of Skye. The Old Man of Storr, or Bodach an Storr as it is correctly known, is a basalt pinnacle that thrusts 160 feet above a hillside that is already some 2,300 feet above sea level. Scientists claim the Old Man is the result of a landslide aeons ago, which is probably accurate but not tremendously exciting. The legends give different accounts. According to one old tale, the

Old Man is the thumb of a giant who is buried underneath the hills. He, or she, must have been some size!

However, there is also a story that the Old Man and one of his slightly smaller companions were two giants, man and wife. They were being chased by some unknown enemy and looked behind them, which turned them to stone in a scenario similar to when the Lord changed Lot's wife into a pillar of salt.

Yet another tale involves brownies rather than giants. According to this version, a local man known as O'Sheen saved a brownie's life without asking for a reward. The brownie never forgot, and when O'Sheen and his wife died, he sculpted the Old Man and the smaller rock in their honour.

And finally, there is the story involving the fairies, who had to get in on the act. This story again has a man and his wife as central characters. Every evening the pair climbed the hill until old age prevented the wife from making the journey. At that point the local fairies stepped in, saying they could ensure the couple stayed together. The husband agreed at once, and the fairies turned both into pillars of rock.

The moral of that story is – never trust a fairy!

A SHIELING STORY FROM LEWIS

In the old Highland culture, summer was a pleasant time. Whole families left their winter dwellings to move their cattle to the high pastures, where they lived in shielings. These were small buildings, little more than a temporary hut that held the basics, mainly a bed of heather and little else. The Highlanders and Hebrideans were outdoors people in the summer months.

In Shawbost, in the west of Lewis, around the beginning of the 19th century, two families decided to build their shielings in a new spot. Two cousins, known only as Dark Mary and Fair Mary, were first to move in. It was a pleasant June day when they milked their cows and churned the butter, then sat outside the shieling, knitting and chatting, singing songs and generally relaxing as the long summer evening drew to its end. Eventually, they put a light to the cruisie lamp, preparing for bed, when an old woman walked up to them.

Neither of the Marys knew the woman, which was irrelevant in the Hebrides where hospitality was a tradition. The Marys invited the stranger in for the night, with all three squeezing into the tiny shieling. In the morning, something woke Dark Mary with a start. She sat up in bed, to see Fair Mary lying dead, with a gaping wound in her chest, from which bright blood flowed. The old woman had vanished, but there was the sound of horse's hooves outside.

Darting to the door, Dark Mary looked outside into the fading darkness of dawn. She saw a horse galloping away, its mane flying free. It was a cach-uisge, a water-horse.

Dark Mary buried the body of Fair Mary beside the shieling and never returned. The local people called the place The Shieling of the One Night and nobody has stayed there since.

THE MACCRIMMON SCAR

Many years ago, in the township of Barvas in western Lewis, there was a man named MacCrimmon. He was a fisherman, and one day he saw a seal-woman, fell in love and asked her to marry him. Such things used to happen when humans lived closer to nature than they do now. The seal woman already had a seal man, but MacCrimmon was a handsome, personable man, and she came ashore to be with him.

The two married and settled down happily, with the result that the MacCrimmons became a very fortunate family. Naturally, with a seal women in their midst, they were natural seamen, ready to sail through the wildest storm, and able to locate the most abundant shoals of fish. Every so often, perhaps once a year, MacCrimmon would carry his wife to the sea, where she cavorted in the waves, very happy with life. MacCrimmon would watch, until one day a massive bull seal reared up at his side and attacked him.

Taken by surprise, MacCrimmon had no time to reach for the dirk he wore at his belt and was getting the worse of the encounter when his wife appeared. With a deep scar on his face from the bull seal's tusks, MacCrimmon was sinking to his death until his wife grabbed the dirk and killed the bull seal.

The seal wife helped MacCrimmon home, telling him that the bull seal was her old lover. From that day on, every Barvas MacCrimmon was born with a scar on his face, and the sea could not drown them.

Generations later, the First World War broke out, and the Hebrides and Highlands poured out their best to fight against the Kaiser's mighty army. By 1917 the war had ground on for three hellish years, three years when Scotland's finest died in their tens of thousands. An officer in a Highland battalion – perhaps the Seaforth Highlanders - knew of the story of MacCrimmon's scar and found he had a MacCrimmon in his company. After a few questions, he discovered the soldier was from Barvas, but, disappointingly, lacked the scar. MacCrimmon was not a great soldier, although he did care for the battalion's pet fox terrier. After a period in the lines, the battalion withdrew to the reserves, being billeted near a private zoo. A leopard escaped, entered the battalion's lines and snatched at the fox terrier. MacCrimmon fought back, lost the dog but gained a scar, which, strangely, followed the same lines as that traditionally worn by his family.

Although saddened by the loss of his dog, MacCrimmon was delighted to have his family scar. After a spell in hospital, he became a model soldier, but, unfortunately, a German shell or bullet killed him. His officer bent to the terrible task of writing to his next-of-kin and asked another Barvas man in the company for details. The man, a MacDonald, shook his head.

"He wasn't a MacCrimmon, Sir," he said. "He was a MacIver, but both his parents died so old man MacCrimmon brought him up as one of his own."

And that, according to MacDonald, accounted for the lack of the traditional scar.

THE SPIRITS OF ABERLOUR

THINK of the images of Scotland – whisky, shortbread, history, river fishing and myths. Now place all these factors together and put them in a village situated on the fringes of the Highlands, add a dash of beauty and a pinch of friendliness, a scatter of unique local shops, and there you have Aberlour.

The full name of the village is Charlestown of Aberlour, named after Charles Grant of Wester Elchies who founded this pretty, prosperous place in 1812, which is nearly modern by Scottish standards. At that period there was a great deal of reorganising going on in the country with landowners creating planned villages all over the place. Charlestown of Aberlour was one of these, a settlement with a broad main street and regular plan, quite unlike the earlier settlements it replaced.

Lying peacefully beside the southeast bank of the famous River Spey, Aberlour could hardly boast a better position. It is easily accessible, with the A95 road carrying traffic past both the Aberlour Distillery and Walkers Shortbread factory. Visitors throng to the distillery tours in summer, anglers head for the majestic Spey, and hikers hitch up their packs and tramp along the Speyside Way or toward the Cairngorm Mountains only a few miles away. However, there is hidden history as well, tales of water spirits and old Celtic saints, of unique people and disadvantaged orphans. Not all is as it appears in this smiling village by the Spey.

Many centuries before Charles Grant made his bid for immortality, there was a small well beside the burn known as the Lour. With the advent of Christianity, this well adopted the name of St Drostan, a follower of St Columba and, around 900AD, St Drostan's Church was built nearby. As so often in Scotland, a settlement grew around the church and came to be known as Skirdustan, a strange, Eastern-sounding name for the heart of Gaelic Scotland but one that means "the division of Dustan" or Drostan. In other words: Drostan's land.

The well and settlement were very close to the Lour, which is a Gaelic word that translates as chattering. The spot where this chattering burn meets the River Spey became known as Aberlour, the confluence of the Lour and, in time, that name replaced Skirdustan. Now there is an excellent whisky distilled on the banks of the Aberlour. My wife's favourite, as it happens, smooth as snow on the flanks of Ben Rinnes, subtle as a seer's sayings and so sweetly scented that angels would sin for a single sniff.

But Aberlour is like that. As I said, nothing is quite what it seems.

There are legends aplenty in this area. Even before Drostan arrived, Celtic druids considered the Lour a sacred place. Legend has it that they thought this burn had healing powers and believed its chattering was the water speaking to them. Apparently, the druids built a shine at a place now known as Fairy Hill, where they talked to the Lour's spirits. The druids are long gone, but there are still names for the strange holes that the burn formed during its tempestuous rush to the Spey. There are several linns, or waterfalls, including the Linn of Ruthrie that rips over ragged rocks to create a mysteriously deep pool, and further upstream is the Little Linn, which surges along a stone shaft at a speed that can be impressive, especially after heavy rain.

While the druids may have worshipped this burn, there are darker tales of a less-than-friendly spirit that expected annual tribute in the form of human sacrifice. Such supernatural beliefs were common in Scotland with an old Border rhyme commemorating the yearly toll taken by the rivers Tweed and Till:

> *Says Tweed to Till*
> *"What gars ye rin sae still?"*
> *Says Till to Tweed*
> *"Though ye rin with speed*
> *And I rin slaw,*
> *For ae man that ye droon*
> *I droon twa."*

The Dee also has its rhyme:

> *"Ravenous Dee*
> *Yearly takes three."*

Today this tribute is less costly in lives as the Aberlour Distillery pours the first cask of each distillation into the burn. There is a story, possibly apocryphal, that one distillery manager halted the practice. Not long afterwards, he was fishing where the Lour merges with Spey and he died there and then. It is best not to make a tradition or break a tradition, or to argue with the old water spirits.

There is more water-lore in the Lour. Over aeons, the

action of the water, possibly augmented by the pebbles it carries, has smoothed out hollows in the river bed. Local people have named each one according to its appearance and character. One is called the Kail Pot – kail, or kale, was a one-time staple of the Scottish diet. Another is the Cups-And-Saucers and a third, the largest of them all, was named the Devil's Punchbowl. One does not have to travel far in Scotland to find some reference to Auld Hornie. He lurked at the edges of consciousness, awaiting recognition in the shape of a rock formation or a hollow in the hills. Aberlour was no different from other places in this devilish nomenclature.

However, the Spey, as well as the Lour, features in local lore. Like the Lour, Spey demanded her victims – and I used "her" with care, for people regarded Spey as feminine. Spey is a moody, capricious river, subject to sudden floods and greedy for human life. Sometimes the spirit of the Spey took the form of a kelpie, a white water-horse that appeared beside weary travellers as they approached one of the fords across the Spey. People seldom saw him, but when the weather was coarse, and thunder echoed from the hills of Cromdale and hammered at the Cairngorms, local people heard the horse's shrill whinny. It was on such nights that the White Horse of Spey sought his prey, searching for beleaguered travellers who wished a quick passage across the fords. The ignorant or the innocent accepted the invitation and clambered on the kelpie's back, only to be drowned in one of the deep pools. The Spey demanded one victim a year as a tribute, perhaps with the kelpie as the personification of the river-spirit.

The Mill Ford lay about a mile or so upstream from Aberlour at the old mill of Easter Elchies. This ford was popular for, except in times of spate, it was sufficiently shallow to be forded on foot, and it was on the traditional route from Elgin to lower Strathspey and the high road south. There is one classic tale that relates how a souter – a shoemaker – named Davie Stuart and his wife Janet were returning from Elgin with a load of leather. It was nearing midnight when they approached the Mill Ford, and they rested before the dangerous crossing.

As they gathered their strength, the Stuarts saw what they believed was the miller's horse grazing nearby, so they jumped on to cross the ford. About halfway across the horse changed direction and began to walk downstream. Only then did the souter and his wife realise that they were astride the kelpie. They struggled to get off, but the kelpie's unholy power held them in place, singing to them.

> *'Sit weel, Jannety and ride weel Davy*
> *The first landing ye'll have will be in*
> *the Pot of Cravie.'*

As the Pot of Cravie was a notoriously deep pool, the souter and his wife knew the kelpie intended to drown them.

Other versions of the rhyme were similar:

> *And ride weel Davie*
> *And by this night at ten o'clock*
> *Ye'll be in Pot Cravie*

Or

> *Ride you*
> *Ride me*
> *Kelpie*
> *Creavie*

"Lord preserve us!" Janet said, and immediately she mentioned God's name, the kelpie disappeared. The couple were floating in mid-stream, wet but saved by the name of the Lord. The water of Spey did not even dampen a Bible that Janet had bought in Elgin.

There is a vague memory of a 17th-century landowner who used to judge witches by the simple expedient of throwing them in the Spey. He sat comfortably on a rock in mid-stream, had them tossed into the water and watched as they struggled. Those that reached the shore were deemed innocent. Those who drowned were obviously guilty. It was not quite a sacrifice to the Spey but not far off.

The mill at Easter Elchies has its own stories, including one about a miller named Saunders Stewart. According to the tale, a local minister heard that his new-born son would drown while a child. Naturally concerned, the minister ensured that the baby never left his side, even when he was touring his parish and giving valuable advice to his flock.

Back then, millers had a bad reputation for overcharging for their services, and the minister visited the mill to give a heated sermon about such practices. He got so carried away with the subject that he let go of his son, who crawled to the mill-lade and was caught by the wheel, thus ensuring that the prophesy came true.

You will remember the water-spirit of the Lour. Well, not far above the present distillery there is the Fairy Hill, and at the farm of Hatton, there is also a cairn and a stone circle, so people used this area well before written history. At one time the cairn or perhaps the Fairy Hill was known as the Shean, which is a corruption of the old Gaelic name of Sidh or Shi – fairy or sacred – and such places were well known to be the haunts of the fairy folk. These fairies could be malicious or friendly, depending on their mood but certainly were never the gossamer-winged creatures of Barrie's Peter Pan or similar stories.

In Aberlour, the fairies used to come down from the Shean to grind their corn at the water-wheel when the miller was in bed. One night the farmer of Hatton was working at the mill, and he did not come back. After a few hours, his wife began to worry that he had slipped in the ford and sent a farm-servant to look for him. The servant saw lights on at the Shean, where a door had also magically appeared. It was open, and the farmer stood just inside, entranced by the fairy music and dancing that he could see.

Fairy hills were like that. They could draw humans in by music and laughter and keep them entranced for days, years or for ever. Tales of alien abductions are not new but, back then, fairies were the abductors and were feared and respected by the humans who shared space with them.

"Come awa hame, Hatton," the servant called (it was common to call people by the name of their farm). "The guidwife is wearying for ye."

The farmer turned around: "Bide a wee, man; what the deil's a' the hurry? Wait till the spring is finished."

In other words: "Wait a minute, there's no rush, wait until the music stops."

But there was no end. The music entranced the farmer and the dancers, the fairies, smaller than humans, played and danced as the farmer clapped his hands to the rhythm.

"Weel dune, little mannie, gang at it wi the little woman." ("Well done, little man, go at it with the little woman.")

Without entering the Shean, the servant could see inside, where the male dancer was dressed in green – the fairy or sacred colour, with yellow knee breeches and blue stockings, while he had silver buckles on his shoes, all colourful to entice the gullible. Grabbing hold of his master, the servant tried to pull him away, but the spell was too strong. The farmer remained.

"Deil ae fit will I gang oot o' this till the spring is finished and the dancing dune."

("Devil one foot will I go out until the music and dancing is finished.")

One year and a day later, the servant returned and this time managed to drag the farmer free, breaking the spell. As was usual in these cases of fairy abduction, the farmer had no idea how long he had been in the Shean, thinking it only a few moments.

Fairies and water-spirits were not the only superstitious beliefs in old Aberlour. Second sight was reasonably common, with one repeated occurrence being the sighting of hearses outside houses days or weeks before a death took place. My Donside grandmother had a smattering of the gift – or the curse, depending on one's point of view. It could not be regulated or explained. It happened from time to time, and that was that. People also feared the evil eye, taking such precautions as placing a crooked sixpence at the bottom of a drinking glass.

Many birds carried ill luck. Magpies (pyets in Scots) were seen as a warning of death or bad luck, while a cock crowing at midnight was a sure sign of bad news. Even the local landowners, the Grants, had a spirit guardian known as Maggie Mulloch, who would appear to warn them if danger threatened.

The old graveyard around St Drostan's Kirk had its own stories. There was once a watch-house where men stood guard to ensure grave-robbers did not dig up the recently interred to sell to anatomists. One day Johnnie Dustan and Jamie Gordon were watching over the grave of a suspected witch when something black and horned knocked them both over. The men fled, convinced that the Devil had come to claim his own. However, when daylight came, they saw a goat grazing among the tombstones.

More sinister is the story a local man told me of the minister who drowned himself in the baptismal font. Unfortunately, I have no more details of that tale, although the font stands proudly in the graveyard. The remnants of the old kirk also still stand concealed behind the leaves of a tree.

With all this supernatural activity around the spirited village of Aberlour, we could expect some outstanding people. Well, we would not be disappointed. As well as Saint Drostan, there was Robert Duff, who repaired the old – and still standing – Packhorse Bridge in 1729 for the princely fee of £5. There was also Bonnie Prince Charlie, who forded the Spey without any mention of kelpies, and did not stop, much to everyone's relief. Free advice: keep well away from kings, princes and politicians for they will all use you to advance their cause. Prince Charlie spent that night in comfort at Thunderton House in Elgin while his followers camped in the rain at the churchyard at Knockando. Not long after, many were dead, lying on the bloody heather at Culloden while the prince escaped to enjoy a drink-ravaged old age.

Nearby is Ballindalloch Castle, once home to WE Johns, who wrote the famous *Biggles* books about a First World War flying ace. The castle was owned by Sir George Macpherson-Grant who spent a lifetime enhancing the Aberdeen Angus breed of cattle. There was also the Reverend Canon Charles Jupp who founded a celebrated orphanage in the 19th century. The orphanage started in a cottage with space for "four motherless bairns" but through Canon Jupp's fundraising – he became known as "The Beggar of the North" – within a few years, his funds built a building that held 30 orphans. Within seven years Jupp had expanded the number of orphans to 100. The orphanage had a farm, church and school but now there are more modern methods of looking after children. However, the charitable notion remains intact with the Aberlour Child Care Trust.

Another notable person associated with this remarkable village was Margaret MacPherson Grant. Born in 1834 as the daughter of an Aberlour doctor, Margaret inherited her uncle's fortune from land and property in Jamaica and London when she was 20. The Jamaican wealth derived from estates that had, until the practice was abolished, used slave labour. Margaret moved into the grand house her uncle had built a mile or so from Aberlour and immersed herself in the Episcopal Church, as well as salmon fishing in the Spey. At a time of strict morals, Margaret pushed the boundaries when, aged 30, she formed a close friendship with another woman, 22-year-old Charlotte Temple from Wiltshire.

Eventually, Charlotte moved in with Margaret, who made her heir to her fortune. But Margaret became a drinker, sometimes consuming more than a bottle of brandy a day. Heavy drinking was far from uncommon in the Victorian period, but one woman going through a form of marriage to another was not. They made a mutual promise of celibacy and Margaret slipped a ring on Charlotte's marriage finger and called her "Charlie", while Charlotte reciprocated with "Jamie" and referred to herself as "wifie".

Throughout this then-unusual relationship, Margaret gave massive sums of money to charity and ran her Jamaican estates without ever visiting them. It may have been a combination of alcohol and the fact that Charlotte became engaged to a man that finally unhinged Margaret's mind. She died aged 42 yet, for all her idiosyncrasies, people remember her best for donating thousands of pounds to help build St Margaret's Episcopal Church in Aberlour and as one of the first benefactors for the Aberlour Orphanage. She deserves to be remembered.

Today Aberlour is a haven in Moray, a village with a broad

main street, an impressive parish church, a unique history, a distillery and shortbread factory and some of the loveliest scenery anywhere. For such a small place, it has a significant number of legends and characters. It is blessed – as long as the water spirits remain bottled.

FORGOTTEN FINDLATER CASTLE

There is a ghost, of course. There is usually a ghost in a Scottish castle, often of a piper or a white or green lady. Findlater's spectre is slightly different. The story goes that a nurse was looking after the toddling heir to Findlater when he became restless. Despite the nurse's frantic attempts to hold him, the baby wriggled out of her arms and fell out of the window. When he landed on the rocks far beneath, the nurse leapt after him. It is a tragic little story that is entirely plausible when you take one glance at Findlater's location.

Many of Scotland's castles have dramatic situations, and Findlater is no exception. Perched high on a clifftop promontory, it crouches in splendid isolation facing the turbulent grey rollers of the Moray Firth. The view is spectacular, extending east and west along a savage coast and northward as far as the eye can see.

A bracing three-mile walk west of Cullen and a mile north of Sandend, the ruins of this once-formidable fortress crown 50-foot-high cliffs. Gaunt, windy and desolate, Findlater is a romantic poet's dream. One imaginative observer termed Findlater "a miniature Gibraltar" which is accurate if you replace the Barbary apes with rock-strutting shags and accept the raucous screams of whirling seagulls. The sea, too, is different, with the blue water of Gibraltar's strait replaced by the splintering grey-and-white hammer of the North Sea.

If a visitor views the castle from beneath, with the sea heaving and churning against the sheer wall of the cliff, he will realise that Findlater was partially carved from the rock itself, with a central block descending into the cliff. The outer walls of the castle are virtually sheer with the cliff, with the lower rooms dug deep into the rock so, in places, the castle could nearly be described as a cave dwelling. Of course, the custodians and owners made the building as comfortable as they could with plastered walls and ceilings, now mostly lost to wind and weather. The rooms were vaulted and, unlike many Scottish castles, boasted large windows, looking out to sea. In winter, this must have been a cold, stark place in the days before affordable glass, so a hardy breed of women and men lived here.

With the castle on a peninsula, sea thundered against the cliffs on three sides, with only a small land border on the fourth. There were ravines cut into the promontory, with two drawbridges for access, both of which the garrison could remove if an enemy threatened. It appears that there was an outwork at the neck of the peninsula, a double defensive rampart for the castle. There would have been buildings between these outworks, stables and storehouses for the castle garrison but even so, this would be a stern, if secure, place to live except during the balmy days of high summer.

Findlater Castle is not on the main tourist trails and escaped much of mainstream Scottish history. Mary Queen of Scots passed by without stopping, King Robert the First did not shelter behind these walls, and Bonny Prince Charles did not hide here while redcoats were scouring the hills for him and his men. That is not to say that there is no history here – on the contrary, this remote castle has many tales to tell.

Some tales are pure history, and some are legend. For example, there is the strange little tale of Sir John Gordon, a 16th-century lordling who was not on good terms with his wife. Or perhaps it would be more accurate to state that he liked to play the field and saw another woman he wanted more. According to the story: "He caste hys fantasie upon another." If the account is even half accurate, his fantasy was as far removed from reality as it was possible to get, for his favoured "other woman" was none other than Mary, Queen of Scots.

With his unfortunate wife confined in a "close chamber" somewhere in Findlater, Sir John was disappointed when Her Majesty marched her army "harde by the howse of Finlitter" without even stopping to shake Sir John's hand, let alone anything else he might have. So much for fantasies. Reality and truth proved bitterer. Alas for romance. Sir John Gordon was the son of the Fourth Earl of Huntly, the so-called Cock of the North. Rather than visiting the queen in her bed-chamber, Sir John had joined his father in rebellion against her and refused to hand over Findlater and his other castle of Auchindoun. He paid for that act of defiance with his head. It is to be hoped that his wife was released from her prison after her wandering husband was out of the way.

The name Findlater seems to come from the Gaelic fionn, meaning white and leitir, cliff, so white cliff. That name would not at first make sense as the cliffs here are browny-green, but they do hold some quartz, and in certain lights, they alter their colour to an approximation of white. It is not an old castle as Scottish castles go, for it does not appear in documented history until as late as 1246. King Alexander III had Findlater, together with other coastal castles, repaired in the 1260s when

Scotland was girding up her loins in preparation for the next, and as it transpired last, war with the Norse. That war ended in Scottish victory when the Norse fleet of King Haakon IV sailed into a squall in the Clyde, and several ships were cast ashore. The waiting Scottish army defeated the Norsemen at the Battle of Largs and in the resulting Treaty of Perth in 1266 the Hebrides passed back to Scottish rule. As they were *de facto* under the control of Gaelic-speaking chiefs, they had been only nominally Norse for decades, if not centuries. However, it was good to have these things tied up legally.

As far as Findlater was concerned, it seems that some of Haakon's warriors occupied the castle for a while before returning to Norway There are no stories or legends of their time here so the Norse could not have made much of an impact.

These early years of Findlater remain a historical blank with not even stonework to recall images. Most of the remains belong to the castle built in the first half of the 15th-century, with Sir John Sinclair of Findlater as the builder. Sir John fought in the 1411 Battle of Bloody Harlaw when the Lowland knights and their followers faced the truly ferocious army of the Lord of the Isles in one of the most savage battles that even Scotland endured.

There are rumours that Sir John Sinclair used Rosslyn Castle in Midlothian as a blueprint for Findlater, and there are vague similarities as both crown a clifftop. As the Sinclairs owned both properties, that scenario is possible, but why travel so far south for a model to build on a naturally defensive site?

In 1437 Sir Walter Ogilvy of Auchleven married Margaret Sinclair, daughter of Sir John Sinclair of Deskford, and Findlater passed to the Ogilvies of Deskford and Findlater. Eighteen years later, King James II granted Sir Walter Ogilvy permission to enlarge the castle, and presumably, some remaining building work dates from that period. The Ogilvies lived here for some time, possibly also with a townhouse or manor house in nearby Cullen. In 1482 the Ogilvies expanded their lands to include Findochty (locally pronounced Finechty) and Seafield. According to legend – and Scotland is never loth to twist a good legend into a historical account – after the infant heir tumbled from the window, the Ogilvies moved home, bag, baggage and bounty, to Cullen. Turning from the sea, they settled in more congenial accommodation a mile or so inland. The move was genuine, but the motivation seems unlikely, although it is a good story.

The legend of Sir James taking a fancy to Queen Mary is indeed a pure fantasy, or rather, twisted history. The reality is convoluted and as cynical as anything that even modern politicians could devise. In the 1560s, the owner of Findlater, Sir Alexander Ogilvy, fell out with his son, James Ogilvy. Sir Alexander disinherited James, granting the castle to his son-in-law, Sir John Gordon, the third son of the Earl of Huntly. James, however, was not a man to watch his inheritance slide away. He was steward to the queen and persuaded her to visit Findlater, which she tried to do. As the Gordons were then in rebellion, Sir John Gordon remained loyal to his father and refused Her Majesty entrance. Naturally annoyed, the Queen sent some of her men to take the castle, but the defences proved too formidable and repelled the queen's army. When the royal forces captured Sir John at the Gordon defeat of Corrichie, Queen Mary granted Findlater to Sir James Ogilvie.

A slight variation of this story claims that Queen Mary asked for the keys to the castle and Sir John Gordon slammed the door in her face, adding injury to insult by ambushing and wiping out a patrol of royal soldiers. Queen Mary retaliated by ordering Sir John to surrender. Rather than that, he took part in the battle of Corrichie, was captured and executed at Aberdeen.

However, there is no doubt that the Ogilvies left for Cullen House. Work on Cullen House began on 20 March 1600 on another impressive site on a high rock above a burn. The original house was a four-storey tower, which extended over time to a complex building of some 386 rooms, one of the largest in Scotland. Today, it has been divided into 11 separate properties. The gardens are still magnificent.

In 1638 James Ogilvy was elevated to become Earl of Findlater. Already Findlater Castle was abandoned and was allowed slowly to decay and gradually tumble into the sea.

There is space for one last anecdote from the Earls of Findlater that shows that the old spirit remained despite the far more luxurious surroundings of Cullen House. In 1791 the Earl expected another local landowner, Brodie of Brodie, to visit. Brodie was very late and apologised, saying he had been attending the launch of a smack – a small sailing vessel – in Aberdeen. The smack was named *Duchess of Gordon*.

At that time, the real Duchess of Gordon was something of a character. Known as Bonnie Jean or The Recruiter, she would not long after this time help her husband, the Duke of Gordon, raise the Gordon Highlanders. In those days, men joined the army by accepting the King's Shilling, and Bonnie Jean helped matters along by placing the shilling within her lips and offering a free kiss to each recruit. Bonnie Jean had been born Jane Maxwell and had a wild reputation. Her father lost his lands and fortune, so Jean's mother took over the education of her children. Jean once rode a pig down Edinburgh's High Street just for the fun of it, laughing at the amazed expressions of the burghers. She lost a finger when she was 14, and always wore gloves to disguise the fact she had one wooden finger as a replacement. Stuck in a loveless marriage with the womanising Duke of Gordon, Jean was so beautiful that there were songs and poems written about her. As her husband had affairs, so did Jean, and always wore tartan despite, or perhaps because, it was outlawed. However, she had a nasty side.

Now the Earl of Findlater was in dispute with Bonnie Jean over fishing rights, and he was to see her unpleasant side. He heard Brodie of Brodie talking with great enthusiasm over this beautiful new coastal smack, which had a copper bottom which would enable it to fight ship-worm as well as protecting the hull when she rested at low tide in the small Moray Firth harbours.

The Earl of Findlater listened intently, thought about his ongoing dispute and commented: "Weel, Brodie, I aye kent that your Duchess had a brass neck and a brazen face, but I never kent she had a copper bottom."

After the ensuing raucous laughter, Brodie left Cullen House. Unfortunately, he repeated the story, which eventually reached the ears of the Duchess. She was not a woman to cross and sued the earl for slander in the House of Lords. Rather than lose his fortune, the earl retreated to Dresden in Germany where he lived out his life.

As can be imagined because of the location, access to Findlater is not as easy as it would be to other, better known, Scottish castles, but the rewards are great for those hardy souls who are not averse to effort. From the west, there is a high-level cliff track from Sandend to the Barnyards of Findlater. From the east, it is a bit of a hike from Cullen with some scrambling, spectacular views and always the possibility of seeing wildlife. This coast has seals and the occasional pod of dolphins for the fortunate. Sometimes whales can be seen, but I'd advise visitors to watch their feet on the path, particularly in coarse weather. There is a more accessible and shorter path from a small car park half a mile or so to the south, but every route will end with a precarious sliding descent from a footpath to the actual castle.

Visitors are advised not to enter the ruins, particularly if they bring children.

When not gasping at the castle or the view, take a few moments to view the Findlater Doocot, which has been here since the 16th century. A doocot, as you probably know, is where the pigeons – or doos in Scotland – were kept to be used as food. This particular doocot is of the beehive variety and held 700 birds: some local wild pigeons still call it home since its restoration in 1992. It may not be as spectacular as the castle, but it is standing history and was remarkable in its day.

As you leave the castle, look behind you. Can you see the ghost of a woman and child on the beach below? Or is that just imagination caused by the surging adrenalin of the walk and the sense of drama that this castle inspires?

THE GHOSTS OF SPYNIE PALACE

Although King William the First created a rampant lion for his royal banner, it is unusual to meet such an animal walking around the Scottish countryside. Indeed, I can honestly say that in my 60-odd years of perambulation, I have never encountered a wild lion. Deer, squirrel, otter, wildcats, pine marten and sundry wild people, yes, but never a lion. Yet a lion stalks the ruins of a former palace within a few miles of Elgin in Moray. Even stranger, the lion is not alive, but a ghost. The lion haunts a gaunt ruin that was one of the most prestigious addresses in Scotland and the home of the Bishop of Moray. That place is Spynie Palace.

Spynie was not always palatial. At one time it was simply referred to as Spynie Castle, which is precisely what it looks like. It sits a bare quarter mile or so off the A941 road from Elgin to Lossiemouth, the former fishing town that is now more geared to tourists and RAF personnel. Despite its prominent position and its place in Scottish history, Spynie is not always easy to find – the motorist has to look for the signpost and should be prepared for a sudden turn on to a minor road. It is a sobering reminder that history can discard even the greatest, for what was once the second most important ecclesiastical palace in Scotland is now a hollow shell.

The Bishops of Moray used Spynie Palace as their seat for five centuries of prayer, feud and manipulation. From its foundation in the 12th century, it was an important place, visited by kings, queens, prelates and commoners. It saw fire and sword and served as a sanctuary in times of war. It hosted the great and the good, the definitely bad and the infinitely worse. Many of the names that loom through the bloody murk of Scottish history put head to pillow here or drew a glittering sword, and some left their mark in the spiritual essence that surrounds this strange place.

In the 13th century, the bishops of Moray transferred their august presence from nearby Kinneddar to Spynie, and from that time onward successive bishops added to the fabric of the building. Today, Spynie Palace stands on flat ground a long stone's throw from the shallow, reed-lined glitter of Spynie Loch, but in the middle ages, the building was on a spit of land that probed into the water. In those days, the loch was very much more extensive, with an outlet to the sea. It stretched as far as Duffus Castle about three miles to the west, and sea-going trading vessels put in with goods. There was also a village here, presumably to service both the castle with tradesmen, artisans and labourers, and the ships with food and whatever else seamen required. Now, greylag geese overwinter, their calls plaintive and evocative, calling to something deep within to follow them to the cold lands of the far north.

There is a legend of the loch. According to the tale, many years ago there lived a laird near Spynie Loch, possibly Sir Robert Gordon of Gordonstoun. The laird had learned the black arts at Padua University in Italy and seemingly wished to test out his skills. On a frosty morning, he ordered his driver to take his coach-and-four on to the thin ice of Spynie Loch. When the driver hesitated, the laird pointed a brace of pistols at him and threatened him with death if he demurred, or if he dared to look back the way he had come.

Terrified, the driver guided his heavy coach on to the frozen loch, feeling it slide on the smooth surface as the ice gave and cracked beneath the iron-shod wheels. Unable to help himself, he glanced over his shoulder. Two corbies, black crows, sat behind him with their intelligent eyes watching everything he did. Immediately the driver looked, the ice gave way beneath the coach. The coach and the wheelers – the horses closest to the coach – plunged downward and only the leading horses continued to pull.

Cursing, the laird snapped his pistols, to swear again when the damp powder failed to ignite. The driver saw the two corbies alter to their authentic form of two demons, who were known to infest the area, and then the leading horses scrambled them clear of the loch and on to dry land.

By the 15th century, Spynie was a substantial chunk of architecture thrusting into the glittering waters of the loch. It boasted a solid curtain wall and a great hall, defensive turrets with a round tower where the bishop would have his quarters. Now, why would a bishop feel he had to live in such a place? He was a man of God, so would his faith not protect him? Well, no; not in Scotland. The land was full of wild men, and a bishop of God had to be as tough as the rest.

In the 1380s, Bishop Alexander Bur was no parochial prelate. He was a well-travelled man who had been ordained by Pope Urban V at Avignon. He knew the ways of the world, so when Alexander Stewart, the Earl of Buchan and Lord of Badenoch left his wife, Euphemia, Countess of Ross, and sired several children with his mistress, the bishop ordered him to return to the marital fold. Alexander Stewart smiled and agreed to comply while remaining with his mistress. When Bishop Bur aided Euphemia in the subsequent divorce case, which cost Stewart the lands his ex-wife had brought to the marriage, Stewart swore revenge on the bishop. That was only one factor that led to Stewart bringing his private army, his "wyld wykkd Heland men" (wild wicked Highland men), to Moray to devastate the church lands and property. Stewart, otherwise known as The Wolf of Badenoch, ordered his men to torch church property in Elgin and Forres, plus Pluscarden Abbey. It is no wonder that the bishops built strong walls around Spynie.

Ironically, a few years later, King Robert III designated Alexander Stewart as the Keeper of Spynie Castle, a position he held for about a year. Perhaps that was when he left something of himself behind, for visitors have seen his ghost there, standing on the first floor of Davy's Tower, staring down at the interior. The only drawback to that theory is that Davy's Tower did not then exist. However, perhaps the Wolf stood within its predecessor, the round tower that occupied roughly the same space.

The 60-foot-high square keep, Davy's Tower was named after its builder, Bishop David Stewart, who raised it some time between 1461 and 1475. Stewart built it for the excellent reason that he was engaged in a feud with the Gordon Earl of Huntly – was it only in Scotland that a bishop could participate in a feud with a powerful nobleman? After the bishop excommunicated the earl, no doubt for excellent reasons, Huntly promised to pull the bishop "from his pigeon holes" which David Stewart took as a threat to destroy Spynie Castle. Accordingly, he replied that he would create a house that could defy the earl and his whole clan. Davy's Tower is the result. At five storeys high and with nine-foot-thick walls, it is a formidable defensive structure, as it had to be, given the times. A century later, Bishop Patrick Hepburn proved his muscular

Christianity when he further strengthened the defences by adding gun-ports in the south and west walls.

If previous bishops seemed a bit less Christian than they might have been, Patrick Hepburn completely thumbed his nose at any pretence of religion. From the day he took over the diocese in 1535, the revenue of the church lands ended in Hepburn's deep pockets, while his people the length and breadth of the country noted his philandering. Indeed, a contemporary writer, Robert Lindsay of Pitscottie said that he "ever was a master of whores all of his days and committed whoredom and adultery both with maidens and men's wives". He was known to have at least five mistresses who, between them, gave birth to 13 illegitimate children. To give credit where it is due, Bishop Patrick took steps to legitimise 10 of his brood. He lived in exciting times with the Protestants attempting to reform the church and the diehard Roman Catholics holding on to their old faith as best they could. Perhaps it was Bishop Patrick who added the indoor tennis court to the palace, and if any bishop had a menagerie, it would be him.

When Mary, Queen of Scots, brought her Catholic faith to the newly Protestant Scotland, there was all sorts of trouble, with Patrick Hepburn up to his overworked middle in it. He altered Elgin Cathedral to make it suitable for Protestants but also supported James Hepburn, the Earl of Bothwell, the alleged murderer of one of Mary's husbands and next in line at the marital altar. A wild man even in those bad old days, Bothwell was a suspected warlock and married Mary eight days after his divorce. He may have influenced his murder trial by positioning a troop of Border riders nearby, lances in hand and swords loose in their scabbards. The people of Scotland could turn a blind eye to much, but were not overly happy with a queen who blatantly married her husband's murderer. They hounded Mary and Bothwell out of sight. Mary ended in English captivity while Bothwell fled north to Bishop Hepburn's care at Spynie. The bishop was his grand-uncle, after all.

Bothwell did not stay long at Spynie but headed for Scandinavia. He ended up chained to a pillar in a noxious Danish dungeon. He died insane after 10 years of foul treatment. In 1567 the Privy Council, Scotland's parliament, ordered that the lead from Spynie Palace roof be removed and sold to improve their embarrassing cashflow problem. The bishop must have thought he had displeased somebody up there, somehow. By now, Patrick Hepburn was well out of favour. He remained in Spynie without his religious rank until he died in 1573 –; he was the last Catholic Bishop of Moray. His financial scandals and sexual endeavours were well known, but now the less-than-good bishop was also accused of studying black magic and summoning demons and spirits from hell. Is there any truth in the claims? There is no doubt that he was not the best bishop in the world, and many people who visit Spynie claim to have seen him haunting the palace, while others mention a very dark sensation that creeps over them when they visit. With the warlock Bothwell, the demon-worshipping bishop and the notorious Wolf of Badenoch in the same building, it is perhaps no wonder Spynie can have a strange atmosphere.

In 1590 the castle and lands were handed to Sir Alexander Lindsay, who became the Lord Spynie. As so often in Scotland, he liked a good argument, but so too did others and when he got involved in a brawl in Edinburgh, somebody shot him. Spynie was indeed home to a collection of interesting people.

There was quiet for a few decades, and the old stones of Spynie may have thought that peace had come to Moray. Unfortunately, war waited just beyond the horizon with the usual twin excuses of power and religion to drive the dark forces. In 1645, The Marquis of Montrose led an army of Ulster MacDonalds and mixed Scottish clans, fighting for the Episcopalian king against the Presbyterian Covenanting government. Montrose had smashed the Campbells at Inverlochy and now marched through Moray "charging all men betwixt 60 and 16 to rise and serve the king under pane of fyre and suord". However, most Moray men wished to keep well out of the way of dynastic disputes. They fled to the stout walls of Spynie for shelter, together with their womenfolk, children, livestock, goods and chattels.

Montrose's men did not attack Spynie castle, and there was no more excitement until 1698 when shingle closed the entrance to the loch so ships could no longer trade. Spynie village died. Relocated a few miles north and west, it became known as Lossiemouth, a name it retains. At the beginning of the 19th century, the renowned engineer Thomas Telford drained most of Spynie Loch, leaving only a shallow pond near to the castle. The remainder became some of the most fertile farmland in the country. In the meantime, Spynie palace gradually decayed. Only the ghosts remain, but there are plenty of them.

Augmenting the lion, whose image is said to appear on the photograph of some visitors and who leaves the occasional pawprint as a reminder of his presence, there is a shadowy face that peers out of the windows on the top storey of Davey's Tower. There is no explanation as to who might be its owner, no story attached. It is just a ghostly face.

On the first floor of the same building, visitors can experience a sudden sore head and a feeling of sickness. Again there is no given reason, no memory of any untoward event. Yet there is a quick cure: if the sufferer steps to one side and asks pardon, the ill-feeling vanishes. Evidently, this is a spirit that appreciates good manners.

Other visitors have heard various noises. The sound of bagpipes is the most usual and is common to very many Scottish castles and caves. They could have come from the caterans who followed the Wolf of Badenoch, or the veteran warriors of Montrose. Only a few years ago an experienced medium brought a group of men to stay in the grounds overnight and heard the sound of hundreds of horses. That must be an echo of a very distant past as neither the Wolf's men nor Montrose's were mounted, and the castle was on the banks of an extensive loch. A member of the medium's team woke up with his face scratched as if by some animal – such as a lion, perhaps?

There are more unexplained things – for want of a better word – in and around this much-storied place. Things such as the human skull that blemishes some photographs and the strange cylinder of white mist. The mist moves silently yet can knock a grown man off his feet. Visitors have seen Patrick Hepburn, or something that people believe is the wayward bishop, and the ghost of a mysterious woman standing just within the entrance to Davey's Tower.

This piece started with a roaring lion and will end on a whisper. Spynie Palace is quiet now, serene beside its calm waters. From the outside it appears much like any other ancient ruined castle in Scotland, yet are there others with quite such a quota of wild or wicked men? From the Wolf of Badenoch to Patrick Stewart, to Bothwell and Montrose, this ecclesiastical pile has witnessed more than most and the spirit of something has remained within its stark stone walls.

HAUNTED ST ANDREWS

EVERY TOWN and city of Scotland has a unique atmosphere, but there are two that are so distinctive that the memory lingers in the senses for ever. One is Edinburgh, the capital, the other is St Andrews, on the East Neuk – corner – of Fife.

St Andrews is famous for golf – the name is synonymous with the sport – but there is much more to this small town. Home of Scotland's oldest university – founded in 1410 – headquarters for centuries of the Scottish church, an important centre for pilgrimage, a significant North Sea trading hub in mediaeval times, and now a tourist centre, St Andrews has many strings to her bow.

With so much history, it is not surprising that St Andrews has witnessed some bloody events. The castle saw a prolonged siege in the 16th century, and its bottle dungeon is a gruesome reminder of the not-so-good-old-days. There were martyrs, both Catholic and Protestant, for it was here that the new "heresy" of Protestantism first came into sharp collision with the old-established Catholic faith. There were murders, such as that of

Archbishop Sharp on Magus Moor, and there were the tragedies of lost love and hopeless desire.

In any town where there exists the intense intellectual effort of a university or the profound happenings of a spiritual edifice, something lingers in the atmosphere. When the spiritual and academic combine in a settlement more than 1,200 years old, the shadow left behind can be impressive. St Andrews, like Edinburgh, contains many ghosts, or at least the impression of human experience imprinted on the essence of the town. It is undefinable, but it is there.

Many of these ghosts, or hauntings, are centred on the old cathedral, the focal point of St Andrews for centuries. Slightly to the south and east of the cathedral ruins stands a 108-feet-tall rectangular tower dating to about 1100 AD. The builders intended this tower to hold the relics of St Andrew that supposedly came to the town – then known as Kilrymont – via St Rule and a storm in the eighth century. The tower is named St Rule's.

There is nothing ornate about this building that has defied all the elements for the best part of 1,000 years, but legend claims that at least one ghost haunts the tower. A spiral stone stairway winds up the interior, and on the darkest part, usually on the night of a full moon, a long-dead monk appears to guide the climber to the top. He is a friendly ghost, but can he be connected with the murder of Prior Robert?

That incident occurred back in the middle ages. Prior Robert de Montrose was a kindly man but he was plagued by one of his monks who shamed the order. This man, sometimes known as Thomas Plater, should never have taken Holy Orders for he had no sense of discipline, or truth, or even morality. On one occasion, the Earl of Douglas brought a large following to St Andrew's and Plater seduced, or perhaps raped, one of the ladies. Prior Robert ordered him to be imprisoned, possibly in the bottle dungeon in the castle that served as the bishop's palace.

Even today, this dungeon is a truly terrible place, bottle-shaped and with its only entrance at the narrow neck. Try visiting outside the tourist season, when a chill mist creeps in from the sea and early winter night shadows the castle walls, then imagine what it was like to crouch in the stygian dark, listening to the ocean outside and the rustle of rats in the straw. It would be a living nightmare.

Prior Robert soon forgave his erring monk – whatever the lady thought of the matter – and released him from his confinement. But the monk did not forgive Prior Robert. One night the prior climbed to the top of St Rules to admire the exceptional view over town and country and sea, and Plater followed, stabbed him to death and tossed the body over the wall to the ground far beneath.

Perhaps the helpful monk of St Rules is Prior Robert, but there is said to be another ghostly figure, whose face is seen above the parapet wall, staring. Could this also be the holy Prior, or are there two spectres in that single tower?

Many of Scotland's ghosts are female. Green ladies and white ladies abound, wandering around all over the place looking sad and sorrowful and generally ghost-like. Not to be left out, St Andrews has at least two in that category, a veiled nun and a white lady.

Visitors most frequently meet the white lady in or around the old cathedral cemetery, which is a lovely spot on a summer day but looks just a little different when a November haar chills the air and obscures the outline of buildings and people.

On such a grim day, it is easy to imagine that time has slipped. St Andrews could be a place of thatched and pantiled cottages, without the explosion of motor vehicles and glaring electric lights. Easy too, to see the young, lovely lady with her long dress rippling to the ground and her dark hair beaded by moisture from the mist. Sometimes she wears a string of beads around her waist, but she also vanishes at a small, square tower in the Abbey Wall. This is known as The Haunted Tower.

According to one legend, this lady is the ghost of an attendant of Mary, Queen of Scots, one of the queen's Marys, whose lover suffered execution at St Andrews Castle. The lady waited between castle and cathedral all night until she knew her lover was beheaded, and by morning her black hair was mottled with grey.

Other tales tell of a girl in white lying in a coffin within the Haunted Tower. When, in 1868, local archaeologists investigated the tower, they discovered two skeletons, and people thought they had laid the ghost. One skeleton was a lady wearing white gloves, the story spread, but more mundane opinion suggests that the skeletons were victims of a plague, not romantic lovers. If so, why bury them in a tower?

Meeting the White Lady may not be an entirely unpleasant experience if her description is correct, but catching a glimpse of the Veiled Nun of St Leonard's is quite another matter. This lady frequents one particular street between the gates of St Leonard's and the road known as the Pends. Dressed in black, the lady has a veil across her face and carries a lantern in her hand. If anybody encounters her, she slowly raises the lamp and unveils her appalling face.

It is best to leave quickly. Hundreds of years ago, a lady lived in South Street; young and beautiful, she attracted many men but rejected them all. Higher things than men filled her mind. One young man was persistent, and in time the two became engaged, reluctantly on the woman's part. It looked to be the perfect match – a lovely young woman from Fife and a handsome, well-set-up gentleman from the Lothians just across the Firth of Forth. But the lady was heartbroken. Rather than become a wife, she decided to marry the church and became a nun, so she joined one of the religious houses in St Andrews as a novice.

When her fiancé learned of her decision, he left Lothian, crossed the Forth on the first ferry for Fife and galloped the length of the kingdom. Meeting his intended in-laws, he discovered that they felt the same as he did and told him where the girl was. He hurried to the convent, intending to bundle her away and marry her, there and then. But he was too late. To ensure she remained free of any man, the girl had mutilated her face, slicing off both lips and eyelids, hacking at her nostrils and taking a red-hot iron to her cheeks.

Distraught, the girl's fiancé screamed and fled across the Forth, to commit suicide in Edinburgh. The girl died shortly after, of sorrow perhaps, or maybe from her injuries. Either way, the Veiled Nun of St Leonard's would be an unpleasant lady to meet on a quiet night.

Quietness in St Andrews, however, is relative as it is very much a university town and students are not always renowned for their decorum. There is even the possibility of hearing the phantom piper who vanished while trying to explore a cave in the sea cliffs.

In the olden days before golf became universally popular and tourism brought bustle to the quaint narrow alleyways of old St Andrews, the street now known as The Scores was named Swallow Gait. Behind Swallow Gait, the cliffs that slide to the sea were not tame at all. This coast was notorious for its winter storms and the Witch Pond where the unfortunates were bound hand to foot and thrown into the sea as a test for guilt. Strangely, the witches have left nothing but memories, their bones and a name: Witch Hill. Only the piper haunts here.

Jock, the Piper, was local, from the tiny village of Argyll

just outside the 16th-century Southgate Port – now West Port – of St Andrews. One Hogmanay, he decided to pipe in New Year within one of the West Cliff caves. This cave was known as the Jingling Cove and had a small entrance but burrowed far inside the rock to a large chamber from where more shafts extended into the unknown.

It was a moonless night when Jock entered the cave, and the sound of his pipes was heard beneath Swallow Gait, beneath North Street, beneath Mercat Wynd, Market Street and no further. Silence.

Jock never emerged from that cave, and his wife pined for him. Loyal, as the best wives are, she waited a full year for her man to return and then decided to hunt for him. It was Ne'erday again and, "I'm going to my Jock," she said, plunging into the fatal cave.

Like her husband, she vanished, and if the pipes are sometimes heard on a wild night of shrieking wind and driving rain, her figure can also be seen, crouched outside the long-closed exit of the fatal cave.

Over a century ago, Dean of Guild Linskill calculated that St Andrews had 80 ghosts. He mentioned only a sample in his book *St Andrews Ghost Stories*. One story tells of the phantom coach, which appears to be very old fashioned and is drawn by four black horses.

The black coach was said to be a death omen as it headed towards St Andrews Bay, but more possibly it was a memory of the murder of Archbishop Sharp of St Andrews. This man was a noted persecutor of Covenanters – extreme Presbyterians – and in 1679, on Magus Moor not far from St Andrews, the Covenanters retaliated. They ambushed the archbishop and, as his daughter watched, shot and stabbed him, crushing his skull to make sure.

Travellers have seen the coach on the quiet moor, without

knowing why it heads out to sea. Nor is there a proper explanation of the ghost who drifts up from the beach to the ruined castle exactly where a flight of steps once stretched, or of the black phantom dog that lives in Deans Court, the oldest surviving house in the town.

There is no explanation and sometimes not even a story. But always a shimmering whisper in this ancient town, if the visitor pauses to listen.

PART TWO
THE WITCHES

INTRODUCTION

In mediaeval Scotland, people accepted witchcraft as part of life. Mainstream history mentioned the craft only when it was used for murder or against somebody in high office. We find it occasionally, such as when Janet Douglas, Lady Glamis, the sister of the Earl of Angus who was accused of being a witch and executed by burning in 1537. But, the Reformation brought a vicious edge that religion had lacked before, with the quote in Exodus, xxxii, 18, "Thou shalt not suffer a witch to live," being considered a direct instruction from God. In 1563, under Queen Mary, witchcraft in Scotland became, for the first time, illegal.

As Christian Scotland prepared to battle with herself, different factions used accusations of witchcraft as a weapon. For example, Roman Catholics claimed that John Knox was "a skilful wizard" who had raised the Devil in St Andrews churchyard. In the same period, diehard Protestants responded with the fiction that Catholic bishops had been "cloven-footed and had no shadows". With such attitudes, no wonder there was conflict.

Although persecution of witches and supposed witches continued from the later 16th century to the early 18th, with about 4,000 people executed in Scotland, there were three main periods. These were 1590-1597, 1640-44 and 1660-1663. Even outside these killing years, a casual accusation of witchcraft could lead to a single woman being hauled before an unsympathetic panel to be interrogated and, at worst, executed. One region where witches flourished was Moray.

THE WITCHES OF MORAY

The locals know the memorial stone is there, but most visitors will drive past without noticing. Even people who have lived in Elgin for years may be unaware of its existence, yet it is in plain sight. The memorial is only a few yards from the main Aberdeen road and a dozen steps from rows of retail outlets and domestic garages. Even the name is deceptive. The Order Pot Stone is meaningless to all but those already in the know. Yet only a few centuries ago, this was a place of terror and torture for many women, and of perceived justice for a community that lived in constant fear of the supernatural. The name Order Pot is a corruption of the original version, Ordeal Pot, for on this site was a pool of the Lossie River and it was here that witches and supposed witches were put to the Ordeal by Water.

The explanatory plaque beside the stone was erected in 1890, and reads:

> *This stone was erected by the town council of Elgin to mark the site of the Order Pot, a circular pond about 70 ft in diameter used of old for trial by ordeal. Though popularly*

> believed to be bottomless, it was filled up in 1881, thus falsifying, it is hoped, an ancient prophecy, "The Order Pot and Lossie grey shall sweep the Chanry Kirk away." The original site of the Order (Ordeal) Pot Pool lies some 130 ft north of this site.

In common with many rivers, Elgin's River Lossie has changed its course over the centuries. Where today the Order Pot Stone sits on a stretch of grass, the river once looped here, and on the bank, crowds of people would gather to watch the torment of supposed witches. There seems to be more legend than substance to the history of this spot, but even the legend reveals a dark period in Elgin's history.

As the largest town in Moray, the region of Scotland that lies between Inverness and Aberdeen, Elgin seems to have been at the centre of local witchcraft, and the council books contain references to witches and "charmers". Yet there only appears to be one record of any who endured a ducking in the Ordeal Pool. However, folklore and legend lend credence to that practice.

The town's records for 1560 do mention a payment of 40 shillings to a certain Andro Edie for "the binners to ye wyffis yat war wardit in ye stepil for witches in summer last bypast". That means the council paid Andrew Edie 40 shillings to supply ropes to tie up women accused of witchcraft. Accusations could stem from many things, from a dirty look that fearful people would believe was the "evil eye" to a knowledge of herbs that generations of a family had passed on, mother to daughter, to malicious gossip, jealousy or genuine fear.

There is one written account of a mob using the Ordeal Pot when people accused a woman named Marjory Bysseth of being a witch. One brave man, known only as Master Wyseman spoke in her favour, saying: "I know this woman to have been a peaceful and unoffending one, living in the privacy of her widowhood... what have you further to say against her?"

The unfortunate Marjory, who the account graphically describes as being "dragged through ye stoure" (mud) near the Pans Port and having "her grey hairs hanging loose" was pleading for "pitie, pitie" from her accusers. One man, a friar, charged her with saying her prayers backwards, while others claimed to have followed a hare to her house (popular superstition claimed that hares were witches in disguise). A group of women accused Marjory of killing cattle by putting spells on them.

"Pitie, pitie, I am guiltless of these false crimes," Marjory pleaded.

However, crowds are pitiless things and wanted her blood. A leper appeared and revealed his arm, withered and defaced with sores. He claimed that he had a mild skin disorder until Marjory had given him an ointment, which had made him a leper. Such an accusation suggests that Marjory was a healer.

Marjory cried: "God has forsaken me; the ointment was a gift from my husband who got it from a holy man overseas."

The crowd had heard enough. Grabbing Marjory, they dragged her through Pann's Port and out to the pool. When she again cried for pity, the people answered, "To trial, to trial," and threw her in the water. When she sank, they roared in exultation, but when she rose, arms raised high, there was a sudden silence. There was another cheer, and when she sank "with ane bublinge noise", the crowd shouted: "To Satan's kingdom she hath gone."

The presence of a leper is not surprising as the Order Pot was very close to the Leper House and leper hospital grounds.

If that account is correct, and there is no real proof, it would seem that in the 16th century, witches in Elgin were summarily drowned without any preceding torture. There are more records for witch trials in the 17th century, with Barbara Innes and Mary Collie hauled before the court in the winter of 1662. The women were accused of entering into a pact with the Devil, renouncing their baptism and of witchcraft.

According to the court, James Home, the parish minister had heard Barbara talk to the Devil in the Fryar Wynd, with the Devil calling her "Bonnie Batsy". Barbara had also met the Devil at different places around Elgin and had charmed and cured other women. The verdict was guilty by a majority. The court sentenced Barbara to be strangled and burned outside the West Port on Tuesday 11 November.

Witchcraft was tolerated in Scotland until 1563 when Mary, Queen of Scots, having been brought up in France, passed the Witchcraft Act. This Act stated that witchcraft equated to sorcery and that a witch was a person who had given their soul to the Devil in return for supernatural powers. From that date onward, witches were persecuted and could be executed, as could anybody who associated with them.

Although public awareness of witches increased, witchcraft trials did not become widespread until Queen Mary's son, King James VI, brought home his bride, Anne of Denmark in 1589. The fear of witchcraft that prevailed in Scandinavia undoubtedly influenced James. Known as "the wisest fool in Christendom", James personally oversaw the torture of suspected witches, so Elgin was not alone. The gullible and fearful pursued the vulnerable and unfortunate all across Europe.

The Order Pot remained as a dark and dangerous place until the early 19th century, when John Shanks, who had the unenviable task of taking care of the crumbling cathedral, tipped some thousands of barrowloads of waste into it. The townsfolk filled in the remaining shallow boggy marsh in the late 1880s.

However, Elgin was only one place in Moray where people

hunted witches. Forres, 11 miles to the west, has its own lurid stories.

In the wall outside the Police Station in Forres is the Witches Stone. It has a small notice that tells the reader that witches were rolled down the nearby Cluny Hill in spiked barrels. Wherever the barrel ended up, the Forres people burned the mangled witch. There are various versions of this ludicrous story, one of which states that there were three witches, each placed in an individual barrel and the Witches Stone marked where one of the barrels ended up. There is absolutely no historical evidence for any of these tales.

However, a play written by a man from deepest England inextricably links Forres and witches. William Shakespeare introduced three witches in his fanciful play *Macbeth* in 1606, not long after James VI and I had begun his obsessive assault on witchcraft. The words of the three witches have become synonymous with witchcraft and are perhaps the best known in the whole genre – if that is the right word – of witchery. Who has not heard the following lines?

> *Double, double toil and trouble*
> *Fire burn and caldron bubble*

As far as Forres is concerned, the witches that a howling mob unceremoniously stuffed in a spiked barrel equate to the three mentioned by Shakespeare. Yet Shakespeare did not create the Moray witches from his imagination. He must have had some knowledge of Scottish history to intertwine witchcraft and royalty in the Moray area, although he used the wrong king.

According to what passed for history at the time, in 962 Duff became King of Scotland. His rival, Culen, raised an army to challenge him but was defeated. Shortly after, Duff became ill, and without a strong leader, the country descended into anarchy. When the king was dying, his warriors found a group of witches melting a wax image of Duff at a fire. Without hesitation, the warriors disposed of the witches, and almost immediately, Duff began to recover. When fully fit, he scoured Scotland for the troublemakers, dragged them to Forres and hanged them. Not long after that, Duff himself was kidnapped and murdered, possibly on the orders of Culen, who became king.

This convoluted story may have inspired Shakespeare's *Macbeth*. If so, the Bard would be right to include Forres. In saying that, there is a much later story about this Witches Stone. At one time it was split into three and utilised to help build a neighbouring house: recycling is nothing new in Scotland. However, in this case, the inhabitants of the house were constantly sick and blamed the Witches Stone. When that stone was removed, banded together and returned to its original site, the illness left the house. If that is true, it certainly puts a new slant on things.

As well as Elgin and Forres, other towns in Moray have an association with witchcraft. Keith, a farmer's market town to the east of Elgin, has the Gaun's Pot. This "pot" is a pool of the River Isla right under the present Union Bridge where mobs drowned local witches. There are several stories but once again, more folklore than history. One tale mentions a Keith criminal who was punished by being nailed by his ear to the gallows. But, when he heard that the mob was drowning a witch, he ripped himself free and ran to watch the fun. There is also the Scaur Stone where a man stood as he pushed a witch under the river. Today the water of the Isla is far better used by the nearby Strathisla Distillery.

On the western side of Moray, and arguably better known, is Gordonstoun, home of the prestigious private school that educated members of the present royal family. Rather than elderly witches, Gordonstoun's story centres around a warlock. Sir Robert Gordon was reputed to have sold his soul to the Devil in return for an extra three decades of happy living. Not surprisingly, people called him the Wizard of Gordonstoun. He was born in 1647 so lived through the latter period of witch-hunting, which was dangerous for a man, even a wealthy man. But probably all he really did was to experiment with the chemistry he had learned in Italy. Superstitious locals would regard anybody different as a warlock, and the stories about Gordon grew legs in the telling. Local people thought the round tower Gordon built connected to the caves at Covesea, which already had a bad reputation due to their Pictish inscriptions. Gordon was also said to have no shadow, which is a sure sign of an evil man. The stories continued – people had seen him eating with the Devil and dancing with naked women. The first was unlikely; the second perhaps the product of a jealous mind. He was said to have learned black magic at Padua, a known centre of sorcery. He had captured a salamander and tortured it over seven years until it told him its secrets. Yet unlike the poverty-struck women whom the authorities executed for far less serious offences, Sir Robert was never arrested: status spoke in 17th-century Scotland.

Finally, I will mention that Auldearn, only a few miles outside Moray, had a very celebrated case in Isobel Gowdie. Walter Scott in his *Letters on Demonology and Witchcraft* wrote extensively about Gowdie. He quotes much of her extensive confession, which includes the first mention of covens of witches in Scotland. Gowdie spoke of digging up the corpses of unchristened children to use the body parts in spells, such as the one used to change a hare back into human form:

Hare, hare God send thee care

> *I am in a hare's likeness now*
> *But I shall be a woman even now*
> *Hare hare, God send thee care.*

Interesting. But can a hare talk?

Although most of the sufferers were women, the chief witch pricker – witchfinder – in the Highland capital of Inverness was a person named Paterson. This individual stripped the victims naked, rubbed hands all over them and used a long needle to prick them in various parts of the body until a numb spot – the Devil's mark – was located. Paterson made much money at the trade and later was found to be a woman disguised as a man. Women could be the tormentor as well as the sufferer.

There is no knowing how many people suffered for supposed witchcraft in Scotland, but it must run into the thousands. Even though Queen Mary's Witchcraft Act was repealed in the 18th century, practising witchcraft remained illegal until 1951, with two women in court for related offences in 1944. Even today, there are some dark whispers.

TRIAL OF THE NORTH BERWICK WITCHES

If the East Coast of Scotland can be likened to a face, with Caithness as the scalp, Buchan as the brow and Fife Ness the nose, then the Firth of Forth can only be the mouth. And if we can continue that analogy, then North Berwick must be the lower lip. Which would be quite suitable in the closing decade of the 16th century, for from here came *Newes from Scotland, declaring the damnable Life of Doctor Fian, a notable sorcerer.*

Not that sorcery was unique to North Berwick, nor new to Scotland. Saint Columba himself had experienced a battle of magic with the chief druid of the Pictish King Bridei, while King Duffus was assaulted by sorcery in the 10th century. Add to that the Inverkeithing priest who, in 1282, "led the ring" in a witches' dance. These are only brief examples of a craft which the Celts may have carried from the East and which possibly merged with whatever native rites the indigenous peoples of Scotland practised before the Celts arrived. In any case, sorcery and witchcraft were in some form deeply rooted in the folk culture of Scotland.

There were probably many varieties of the craft, most

being harmless, even benign, as the wise women healed the sick and prescribed love potions to pining young people. Some versions, however, were not. Possessors of the evil eye were feared, particularly in the Highlands, although more for the alleged harm they could do to livestock than anything else. Stories of, and belief in, shape-shifters was common – cats and especially hares being the most common animals that witches could inhabit. Seers were widespread, with the Brahan Seer only the best known of a host of soothsayers, but the second sight was more thought of as a curse than a blessing. And even more evil were those people who practised sorcery with intent to harm.

As late as the 19th century, there was a witch in Orkney who sold favourable winds to seamen, with Arctic whalers frequently utilising her skills. It stands to reason that less well-disposed witches would attempt to raise winds for other purposes. In North Berwick, in 1590 a mass gathering of witches hoped to call up a storm that would sink the ship carrying King James VI back to Scotland.

James VI was one of the most unusual and outstanding kings ever to plant his royal posterior on a European throne. Never a courageous man, James spent much of his Scottish reign in fear of assassination. Yet this continual terror did not prevent him from waging a form of cultural genocide on the Gaelic population of his kingdom. Added to this was his fierce campaign against the Border clans, when the noose, drowning pool and exile removed hundreds of people from the southern counties.

Yet James was fundamentally a man of peace and learning. Not only did he occupy the Scottish throne for 35 years but he also sat on the combined throne of Scotland and England for a further 19. His subtle diplomacy created a single kingdom out of two longstanding enemies and gave England, shockingly impoverished at the end of Elizabeth I's reign, a strengthening peace.

But for all that, James is perhaps best remembered for his interest in, and fear of, witchcraft.

In common with many monarchical unions of the time, James's marriage was more of a duty than a pleasure, but his match with Anne of Denmark was a reasonable choice. Anne's looks and personality balanced James' intelligence and statesmanship. When they set sail from Scandinavia for Scotland, there should have been celebrations in the land or at least confidence in the future.

Not everyone, however, was pleased with the return of the king from Europe, and one of the most displeased was Francis Stewart, Earl of Bothwell, the son of one of James V's illegitimate sons. His mother was a sister of that James Hepburn Bothwell who had so fascinated Queen Mary. But the present's earl's reputation was of dark magic, rapid raiding and a hint of madness. Perhaps it was Bothwell who called the coven to meet at North Berwick, in the old 12th-century church beside the pilgrim's harbour. He certainly got the blame.

David Seaton, a deputy baliff of nearby Tranent, became suspicious of the actions of his maid, Geillis Duncan, who had taken to leaving the house at night, curing the sick and performing "many matters most miraculous". When Seaton asked how she managed to do this, Duncan did not reply, so Seaton gathered up some of his friends to investigate further. After torturing Duncan with thumbscrews and rope, they then searched her for the Devil's mark. As all witches were known to have such a mark, the searchers soon found one.

After that, Duncan confessed to witchcraft. When she was imprisoned and questioned, she listed a whole string of "notorious witches." Her list included Agnes Sampson from Haddington, Agnes Tompson from Edinburgh, Robert Grierson, a ship's skipper, Jennet Blandiland. Euphame MacCalzean, Barbara Napier and Doctor Fian.

There were many others, from East Lothian, Edinburgh and Leith, but the authorities believed the principals were Dr John Fian, Agnes Sampson and Barbara Napier. Other significant witches included Euphame MacCalzean, while Geillis Duncan helped things along by playing the trump or Jew's Harp. Agnes Sampson was "not of the base or ignorant sort of witches, but matronlike, grave and settled in her answers" when she appeared for trial. Despite his fear of witchcraft, or perhaps because of it, King James insisted on personally judging the accused at his palace of Holyroodhouse in Edinburgh. When Sampson denied everything, her jailers took her away, tortured her again and brought her back when she was more pliant. In her second session before the king, Sampson confessed to being the elder witch and revealed what had occurred. Either that, or she told the king what he wanted to hear rather than endure further torment.

"Agnes Sampson confessed that upon the night of Allhallow Eve (Hallowe'en) last, she was accompanied... with a great many other witches, to the number of two hundred, and that they all went to sea, each one in a riddle or cive (sieve)... with flaggons of wine, making merry and drinking by the way... to the kirk of North Berwick in Lowthian."

Sampson claimed that, after they landed, they "daunced the reill... singing all with one voice."

> *"Commer, goe ye afore, comer goe ye*
> *Gin ye winna goe afore, commer*
>   *let me!"*

It was to this reel that Geillis Duncan played the trump, so King James was not satisfied until he had sent for her. The tune may have been a Ring Dance, performed around some fixture, such as a cross or standing stone, or around the Devil himself. In this case, people suspected that Bothwell was acting as the Devil. Whoever the actor was, he was displeased that the witches were late, so "enjoyed them all to a penance... they should kiss his buttocks, in sign of duty to him, which being put over the pulpit bare, everyone did as he enjoyed them".

After that little ceremony, the Devil "did greatly inveigh against the King of Scotland" who he claimed was "the greatest enemie hee hath in the world".

Although that news must have alarmed King James, it could also be construed as a compliment, putting James firmly on the side of good. His much-mistreated Gaelic subjects might have disagreed.

"Now," Sampson said, "if you disbelieve in our power, listen to this," and she told the king the precise words he had spoken to his new queen on their wedding night. This information impressed James, and he listened as Sampson explained how she had tried to kill him.

Collecting the venom from a black toad in an oyster shell, she had hoped to place it on an article of the king's clothing. This manoeuvre would have "bewitched him to death, and put him to such extraordinary paines as if he had been lying upon sharp thorns and endes of needles".

Luckily, the king's attendant, John Kers, refused to supply any clothing to help Sampson. Kers was evidently a loyal man, and brave to deny the request of a known witch.

Sampson also revealed how she had raised a storm that sank a ship in the Forth. To do so, she had christened a cat and "afterward bound to each part of that cat the cheefest part of a dead man, and several joynts of his body" before they threw it into the sea off Leith with a great shout of "Hola!" The ship that sank was carrying gifts to the new queen, but that was not the end of the spell. Sixty people also drowned, but the primary purpose was to raise contrary winds for the king's passage from Scandinavia to Scotland. Only James's faith, claimed Sampson, saved his ship from sinking.

There had been other meetings beside that at North Berwick. At a coven near Prestonpans a "body of wax... wrappit within a lynnyng (linen) claith" was delivered to the Devil before being handed round all the gathered witches. Each witch had to say the words: "This is King James the sext, ordanit to be consumed at the instance of a noble man Francis Erle Bodewell" – that is, Bothwell. In the light of this damning evidence, James ordered the arrest of the earl and continued to examine lesser culprits. One such as Doctor Fian.

Doctor Fian was more commonly known as John Cunningham, a schoolteacher and a man presumably of some importance in the circle of witches since he was the only man allowed to "come to the divel's readings" and was always at his "left elbock" (elbow). Once imprisoned, the authorities tortured Fian until he confessed. His head was "thrawed with a rope" which was an inexpensive torment whereby a cord was bound around the victim's forehead and tightened until the skull cracked and the eyes bulged.

The schoolteacher said nothing, either to that or to "sweet persuasion", so the torturers tried "the most severe and cruell paine in the world, called the bootes." That, and the release of a witch's charm, broke Fian's resistance. The boot was a horrible device that crushed the shinbone and knee cap, so it was hardly surprising that Dr Fian confessed.

Apparently, Dr Fian was present at all the "general meetings" of the witches. He also knew of the plot to kill the king. In fact, he had tried to catch the cat "and she proving very nimble, he was carried about in the air after her in a wonderful manner". Fian added to Sampson's version by adding that

Satan threw some spherical object, "like a foot-ball" into the sea, hoping that James would be cast ashore in England, not Scotland.

But it is perhaps Fian's attempts to use magic for his personal affairs which are more revealing. There was a "gentleman dwelling neare to the Saltpans" who admired the same woman as did Fian, so the doctor cast his spells. This action resulted in his love rival becoming subject to fits. Even in the king's presence, this man "fell into madness, sometimes bending himselfe and sometimes capring (capering)... to the great admiration of his majestie".

With his rival at least partially indisposed, Dr Fian attempted to meet the lady "to obtaine his... wicked intent" but without success. So another spell was needed. One of Fian's pupils was a brother of the lady, and the doctor told him to "procure three of her hairs, by which he might bewitch her." Unfortunately for the pupil, his mother was also a witch – they must have been thick on the ground in East Lothian. She discovered her son at his hair gathering and "did beate him with sundrie stripes" until she forced out the truth.

Unhappy at this attempted seduction of her daughter, the mother cut three hairs from the udder of a young cow and ordered her son to hand them over to the doctor. Fian worked his spell, but instead of the girl, it was the heifer that became lovesick, "leaping and dauncing upon him, and following him forth of the church and to what place he went."

After this confession, Dr Fian vowed to become a Christian, until another visitation by the Devil forced him to abscond from jail. Rearrested in Prestonpans, he denied his previous words, despite further torture. Indeed, he claimed, "that what he had done and sayde before was onely done and sayde for fear or paynes which he had endured." Such a regression could not be allowed, so at the end of January 1591, John Cunningham, Dr Fian, was strangled and burned at Castlehill in Edinburgh.

The witch Euphame MacCalzean was no gullible country girl, but the daughter of Thomas MacCalzean, Lord Cliftonhall of the College of Justices. A court convicted Euphame of attempts to kill the king by witchery, and of trying to kill her husband so she "might get another goodman" (husband). The court also found her guilty of helping to sink the ship in the Forth, and ordered her execution.

Agnes Sampson, known as the wise wife of Keith, was also put on trial. Added to her attempts on the king's life, the court convicted Sampson of "taking up dead folks and jointing them" to make "enchanted powder for witchcraft" and many other witchy things, including using her power to heal people of sickness. One of her spells had this curious line: "All kynds of ill that ever may be, in Christ's name, I conjure thee."

Barbara Napier was another witch from an upper-class background. Previously suspected of being involved in the death of Archibald, the ninth Earl of Angus, it is possible that Napier had been found guilty but paroled because of her pregnancy. This time, the court found her guilty of consulting with the warlock Richard Graham and sentenced her to be executed.

The Earl of Bothwell was arrested and held in Edinburgh Castle, where he protested his innocence. The court convicted him, Bothwell said, on the evidence of the Devil, who "was a liar from the beginning of time". There is certainly logic in that statement.

Before he came before the king, Bothwell escaped to the Borders, where the population did not care if he was the Devil or not. An example of Border morality came when an innocent stranger asked a Borderer whether there were any Christians in the area. The man thought for a while before replying. "Na," he said. "We're a' Elliots and Armstrangs here."

So Bothwell was in good company. Perhaps he was more an opportunist than a true believer in the black arts, but he lived a life of maniacal raids on the king, mingled with borderline murders. Finally forced out of Scotland, Bothwell died abroad, practising as a conjurer. He remains one of the most enigmatic bad men in Scotland's story.

Between 1560 and 1707, more than 3,000 suspected witches were killed in Scotland, mainly women and mostly convicted on the evidence of women. Although many were undoubtedly innocent of any ill intentions, others believed that their actions would do harm. Witchcraft was not a phenomenon peculiar to Scotland. One estimate said that around 100,000 suffered execution in Germany, for instance.

And just about everyone was convinced that witches had the power to raise spells. John Knox took part in a witchcraft trial. James VI in 1597 wrote the *Daemonologie* on the subject. In 1567, Lady Foulis employed a wizard to dispose of her stepson and his wife. When his spells failed, the wizard resorted to rat poison.

Yet it was the trial of the North Berwick witches that began a wave of witch hunts. Other hysterical outbreaks occurred in the late 1620s, the 1640s, 1650 and the early 1660s. After that, the trials became more infrequent and with more possibility of an acquittal.

More tolerant of such things, the Highlanders had very few witch trials. James VI, the arch anti-Gael and anti-witch king, would not have approved.

WITCHES OF THE LOCH

Not all witch stories end in persecution and the gallows noose. A more cheery tale comes from the Lake of Menteith, or the Loch of Inchmahome as it was originally called, from Innis mo Cholmaig, the island of St Colmoc. This loch has another strange story, which claims that the locals used the resident geese to fish for pike. Apparently, the locals tied baited lines to the legs of the geese and set them loose on the water. The pike ate the bait, the geese fought them and eventually landed on shore with the fish, which the humans ate.

Anyway, to return to the witches. When one of the Earls of Menteith was entertaining visitors in his castle on Inchmahome, the main island in the loch, he ran out of wine. Shouting for his butler, the earl sent him to Stirling to buy some more. The butler grabbed an empty cask and rowed from the island to the mainland, knowing he would be very fortunate to get to Stirling and back before the festivities ended. However, the butler happened to see two witches in the reeds at the margins of the loch. He watched as they each cut themselves a bundle of reeds, or perhaps bulrushes, mounted the bundle, shouted,

"Hae wi ye," and flew away. The butler followed suit and flew to the court of the King of France, where he filled his empty cask with French wine.

He returned to the earl with a full barrel of wine plus the King of France's silver drinking cup to prove the veracity of his story. I rather enjoyed that little tale.

THE STORM WITCH

The first time I sailed to Orkney, it was 1978. I was wandering around Scotland, poking into strange places to see what I could find, talking to people, getting into minor trouble and wishing I had more money. In those BC (before Cathy) days I was free and as irresponsible as any unmarried young male.

I was standing at Scrabster harbour, waiting for the ferry and staring into the murk to the north. The sea was breaking green-blue and silver against the harbour wall, sending great sheets of spray and spindrift high into the air, retreating with a sinister hiss and gathering its strength for another assault. I was wondering where Orkney was in the gloom when an elderly man joined me at the rail. My companion was straight-backed, with his face a mass of lines and wrinkles but the bluest, brightest eyes I had ever seen.

"Enjoying the view?" He asked, with a sodden cigarette somehow attached to his lower lip.

"There's not much to see," I said.

"Aye, no' the day. But on a clear day," this old fellow said.

"You can see Orkney." He paused a little, "or so my grandfather told me."

It took a while for the dry humour to sink in, but that was my introduction to Orkney. I found the island group one of the most magical, historical and fascinating of places that Scotland, or indeed the world, has to offer. Perhaps it was the Scandinavian influence that gave the Orkney Isles such a reputation for witchcraft. In the old whaling days, sailors used to land in Stromness and seek out a wise woman who would predict how many whales their ship would catch and sell them favourable winds for sixpence.

Nevertheless, Orcadians did not view all their witches so favourably. Take Jane Forsyth of Westray, for instance. She lived in the 17th century when, as we have seen, witch-hunting was something of a national pastime, and nosey neighbours were only too ready to point an accusing finger.

Jane Forsyth was a young woman, with all the natural desires and wiles a healthy woman should have. Her sweetheart was named Benjamin Garrioch, a farmer from the same island of Westray. It was on a July morning in 1627 when Jane first stepped out of the ordinary. Benjamin and some of his friends were intending to take a boat out fishing when Jane advised them to stay on land.

Young lads were as nonchalant then as they are now and laughed off Jane's warnings, saying that they understood the sea better than she did, and there was no reason for worry. When she realised the lads were intent on fishing, Jane told them that the previous night she had dreamed of them out in their boat, and said a calamity would befall them. Still laughing, the lads said the weather was beautiful and the sea flat calm. As Benjamin launched the boat, Jane wrapped her arms around him, said, "Oh, don't leave me, Ben," but without effect. The four young men pushed out to sea towards the Westray Firth.

And they vanished as if they had never been.

Somehow, news of Janet's warning spread around Westray, and tongues began to whisper the word "witch". After that, life became increasingly difficult for Janet Forsyth. Her father died, leaving her alone in a world where the family was far more important than it is now. Not unnaturally after losing her sweetheart and her father, Janet became depressed, withdrawing into herself and not wishing to talk to anybody. Janet lived in a small cottage, huddled close to the ground, with tiny windows that she kept shuttered against the world and a roof of heather-thatch with a hole in place of a chimney. When she withdrew from society, adventurous boys clambered on to the roof and peered through the smoke-hole, seeing Janet sitting alone and unkempt, with her arms folded as she sang sad songs to herself.

As Janet's depression coincided with a spell of wild weather, people thought she was summoning the Storm King from the depths of the ocean. The people of Westray began to call her the Storm Witch, and their suspicions heightened when Janet eventually left her home. Sometimes, when rough weather kept the other boats beached, she would hurry from her cottage with her shawl covering her hair, and her shoulders bowed against the wind. Rather than seek shelter, Janet would sail out in her father's boat, seeking her man. Her reputation as the Storm Witch was enhanced when she returned safely, again and again.

In such a perilous occupation as fishing in the northern seas, mishaps were frequent, but rather than blaming the weather; the Westray fishermen began to blame the Storm Witch. When a man named Robert Reid became sick, he approached Janet and accused her of putting a spell on him. Probably irritated by all the accusations, Janet doused him with a bucket of sea-water, telling him the soaking had cured him.

Reid's symptoms vanished, and Janet's reputation as a witch grew.

However, witches had a dual purpose in the north, and when sickness struck, the sufferers sought Janet for help. Perhaps she was indeed a healer, or maybe the solution was in the mind, for more often than not, Janet was able to affect a cure. Unfortunately, Janet was also blamed for any sudden death on Westray, particularly of the island's livestock. The more superstitious people accused her of putting the evil eye on their beasts and, unless they needed her expertise, they avoided Janet all the more.

Being islanders, the Westray people at that time lived by the sea, so if the sea chose to hand them a shipwreck, they accepted the gift with gratitude. When one of the frequent storms roared up, and a ship was in evident difficulties off the island, the people gathered in the expectation of reaping a maritime harvest. Nobody ventured out to help the crippled vessel, except of course for Janet.

Now, Westray is not the most accessible of islands, with powerful tides even when there is not a storm, so nobody expected Janet to survive, let alone reach the beleaguered ship. The storm battered at Janet's tiny boat, throwing it up on the crest of gigantic waves, then dropping it so deep into the troughs that it vanished for minutes at a time. The islanders peered through the curtains of spray and spindrift that rose high into the damp air. However, each time Janet's boat appeared, it was closer to the ship until at last, it was alongside, and Janet boarded the stricken vessel. Without hesitation, she took over the wheel, yelled orders and steered to the relative safety of Pierowall Bay.

Rather than accept the thanks of the crew or the reward money the shipmaster tried to press into her hand, Janet left hurriedly, only saying she hoped that somebody would rescue

Benjamin if they ever met him. Without another word, she returned to her cottage, to sit, singing, by the light of her peat fire.

In the 17th century, people were less educated and much more superstitious than they are now. The good folk of Westray saw Janet's actions not as the act of a supremely skilful woman but as the arts of a witch. They had her arrested and tried in St Magnus Cathedral. Her history of curing others was given, with her supposed use of the evil eye and her calling up the Storm Gods. It was nearly inevitable that the court found her guilty, although she proclaimed her innocence and said: "In saving the crew of the vessel referred to, I had no assistance but from God."

The judge ignored her words and ordered that the local hangman tie her to a stake, strangle her to death and burn her body. The audience applauded the sentence. As the applause died away, Janet turned to face the crowd; she looked at a group of seamen, and all the colour drained from her face. She screamed and collapsed, saying: "Save me, Ben!"

One of the sailors leapt forward and lifted her from the floor, holding her close as he murmured in her ear. The judge ordered the sailor to hand back the condemned witch, and for a few moments, it seemed that there might be a battle in the cathedral as sailors and court officials squared up to each other. In the end, the authorities carried Janet to Marwick's Hole, the dungeon in St Magnus Cathedral, to await her fate.

When the day appointed for Janet's execution dawned, the cathedral bell tolled its sonorous message and a crowd gathered, including many officers and ratings of the Royal Navy. The previous night had been one of celebration as there was a significant naval presence at Kirkwall. Only the hangman and his two assistants remained in the condemned cell with Janet.

As the crowd gathered to see Janet burn, the Sheriff-

Depute and the Provost of Kirkwall marched to the cell to collect the condemned witch. They stopped short when they saw that the door was open, the hangman and his assistants both slumped unconscious on the ground, and the main attraction missing.

Witchcraft! The word soon spread around the town. Janet must have used her powers to knock out three muscular men, open the locked door and vanish, for a thorough search of the Orkney Islands failed to find the condemned witch.

And that seemed to be the end of the matter. The Storm Witch had used her powers and was now in hell with her dark master. Or was she?

It was years before the truth came out. Bailie Baikie of Kirkwall was travelling down to London on official business and stopped at Manchester en route. He was surprised to see a shop with the Orkney name Benjamin Garrioch above the door. Baikie was even more surprised when he walked in and found Janet Forsyth, the Storm Witch, managing the premises, looking younger and happier than she had when mourning on Westray.

Naturally curious, Baikie asked for more details. Only when Baikie promised to keep her tale a secret did Janet relate what had happened.

When Benjamin and his friends sailed out that calm day, they were right about the weather. There was no storm. But worse, a Royal Navy warship passed and pressed them all into the crew, where they remained for years. Years later, they were in the fleet that anchored at Kirkwall, and Benjamin was among the seamen who saw Janet condemned to death. Rather than watch his sweetheart burn, Benjamin smuggled rum into Marwick's Hole, passed a bottle to the hangman and his friends, and poured in a sleeping draught.

Freeing Janet and smuggling her away was easy, but

escaping from the islands not quite so simple. However, the captain of the vessel Janet had saved was glad to help and brought Janet on board. As they sailed to Liverpool, Benjamin remained with the fleet that arrived at Portsmouth. He was either paid off there, or deserted, and met up with Janet in Manchester, where they married and ran a very successful business.

And with that happy ending, I will close the section on witches and move on to fairies.

PART THREE
THE FAIRIES

SCOTTISH FAIRIES

OLD SCOTLAND WAS awash with fairy lore. Scottish fairies lived lives much like humans, with an entire community eating, drinking, sleeping and dancing. They wore (or wear, perhaps), bright clothing and used utensils of gold and silver. Green is the favoured fairy colour, while they disapprove of others wearing their colour. Strange – I have met women who refused to wear green because they thought it "unlucky", without knowing why. Folk traditions die hard in Scotland. At the Battle of Killiecrankie, Grahame of Claverhouse, Bonnie Dundee, wore green. He won the battle, yet one of the Williamite soldiers killed him – with a silver bullet, according to legend. The Grahams avoided green after that, or so the story goes.

The fairy folk also steal food from humankind, extracting the *toradh,* or goodness, leaving only the appearance for humans to eat. Have you never wondered why your meal was not satisfying today, and you feel you need to snack afterwards? Well, blame the fairies. That is one of their little tricks.

Highland fairies also had delicacies, such as heather tops,

fresh heather shoots and the roots of the silverweed. They milked the wild goats that were once common in Scotland, and the red deer that still roam in their thousands.

The fairies could be unwanted guests in a house, for they had the unpleasant habit of stealing children and leaving one of their elderly in the cot. Mothers ensured their babies were christened as soon after birth as possible, for fairies could not abduct a baby after the Lord's blessing. One device to repel the People of Peace was to make a Harvest Maiden from the final harvest of grain. The farmer, or his wife, would suspend this little figure in the house to keep the place safe from fairies for the year. Another method was to hang up holly on Hogmanay. And I always thought that was a Christian tradition!

THE FAIRIES OF MONIKIE

Sometimes there are clues to Scotland's fairy lore, although it needs a local key to unlock the secrets. Such a case is in Monikie (pronounced Moneekie) only a couple of miles from where we presently live. It was my son-in-law, Graeme Ritchie, who told me the story or I would never have known of it.

Monikie is an ancient settlement, much expanded by modern housing, right beside Monikie Country Park. At one time there was an inn known as Fiddlers Inn, which has now vanished, although the name Fiddlers remains in a street name that dimly remembers an old legend. The version Graeme told me ran like this. One day two fiddlers came to Monikie from Monifieth, a small town on the coast a couple of miles away. They spent the day and evening playing the fiddle, then walked home to Monifieth, down the slope to the south.

Their shortest route took them across the Laws, which is a prominent group of low hills – laws – that was the site of a Pictish settlement. On one of the surrounding fields was a fairy circle, locally called the Roondie. The fairies, seeing two fiddlers and always keen to hear good music, invited them in for the night. The fiddlers, probably a little inebriated, agreed and entered the fairy circle. They played all night and left at dawn.

However, as with many similar cases, their one night in fairyland had extended to 100 years in real time. When they left the fairies and walked through the streets of Monifieth, they stared at all the differences. Their friends and family were long gone, and when they passed the church, both fiddlers turned to dust. Christianity and the People of Peace, the fairies, were ill bedfellows. The next story is better known.

THE FAIRIES OF EILDON

THEY RISE, humped and alien, dominating the country for miles around. The Romans called them Trimontium – the triple peaks – and rested their legions in their sinister shadow. The three hills of Eildon, not high by any standard but unique where they sit amid the green and breast-swells of Border fields, form a mysterious island of legend and mystery.

The atmosphere here is undeniable, but it cannot be defined. All the Border area of Scotland has a certain feeling, a tension as if waiting for the hoofbeats to sound again as long-gone armies recommence the ancient wars. But not here – these hills hold something older, something not quite eerie but not canny either, something not of this world. Or not of our perception of this world. Here, once beyond the fields, once beyond the smooth greens of the golf course, the world changes. Sometimes for ever.

At the back end of the 13th century, Scotland was a nation at peace. Good King Alexander, the third to bear that name, had defeated the Norse at Largs, waiting until the autumn storms drove the dragon ships ashore before attacking with his army. Since then, there had been peace, Hebrides, Highlands and Lowlands together. A blending time as Dalriad and Pict, Norman, Norseman, Briton and Saxon merged their identities to become one nation. Rather like the 13 colonies in America and all the component races therein. But as always in Scotland, there was the X factor, the unknown, or the unknowable.

Thomas Learmont was the Laird of Ercildoune Tower in the fertile central Borders. It was not a large place, and Thomas was not a wealthy man, but these were the days before an English king's megalomania started the long wars and there was peace to enjoy, and a little prosperity. Peace creates leisure and one morning in May, Thomas was lying beneath a single tree on Huntly Bank, the eastern slope of the Eildon Hills, listening to the chatter of the Bogle Burn, when a lady rode towards him.

All the essentials for romance were there, the young laird, the lonely, idyllic spot and the beautiful lady, but there were also clues to the so-far-hidden meaning of the tale. May morning was as significant a date as Hallowe'en or Midsummer to the Celts; lone trees, oak, rowan, elder, were powerful symbols of the pre-Christian druids, and the lady was wearing green – the fairy colour.

Taken by her beauty, Thomas knelt before her, with the birds singing all around and the tree green above.

The fair lady was Queen of the Fairies and doomed Thomas to spend seven years in Elfhame, having entered "underneath a derne lee" – a subterranean cave beneath a lochan. Once there, Thomas seemed to enjoy himself. There were feasting and dancing, adventure, knights and their ladies, hounds and deer but always the fear that a "foul fiend" would come to claim him. Rather than suffer the unknown fate, the Queen gave Thomas an apple that endowed him with a "tongue that can never lie" and brought him back to Huntly Bank.

Again in Ercildoune, Thomas now had the gift of prophesy, the "second sight" and as Thomas the Rhymer he is remembered. He foretold the death of Alexander III and the Battle of Bannockburn, the accession of a Scottish king to the throne of all Britain and, better remembered, said the words:

> *"Tide, tide whate'er betide*
> *There's aye be Haigs at Bemersyde."*

That was a prophesy I read in a book published in the middle of the 19th century. But not until 1921 was Bemersyde House given to Field Marshal Earl Haig in gratitude for his leadership in the First World War.

But the Queen of the Fairies was not yet finished with Thomas. One day, he knew, he would be summoned back to Elfhame, and when a white hart and hind came together to walk through the single street of Ercildoune, Thomas knew it was the Queen's message for him. He followed the deer, entered the hills of Eildon and vanished. His tower still stands outside Ercildoune, or Earlston as it is known today. Crumbling, decayed, but still there.

That was a nice, neat little fairy story, but how much truth was in it? Scottish fairies were never of the tiny, gossamer-winged variety. They were earthy, robust, often formidable and often tricky. The further back in Scottish history the stories read, the more the presence of fairies is accepted as fact; not with superstitious dread, or romantic fantasy, but as part of the natural order. They existed, they were there, a hazard like wild beasts or foul weather but sometimes a blessing as well as a curse.

The Eildon Hills was only one of the very many fairy hills throughout Scotland, often prominent sites, isolated or shapely, for the fairies had a good eye for country. In Edinburgh, Calton

Hill had its fairy boy well into the 17th century. Aberfoyle on the Highland fringe has an exceptionally well-documented hill where the Reverent Kirk saw the fairies and where he possibly still lives. Tom-na-hurich in Inverness was the reputed headquarters for northern fairies and Schiehallion, which is near enough dead centre of Scotland, was the fairy capital of Perthshire. The very name means Fairy Hill of the Caledonians.

These were the main centres. There are scores more sites of local interest, some of them ancient burial sites, or Druidical sites, such as Calton, or Iron Age forts like Eildon. There is a fort on the eastern summit of Eildon, a cairn on the taller central peak. Both were old before the coming of Rome, and both overlook a fascinating landscape.

From Eildon, the whole central Borders spreads like a map, and on the fringes of the hills, within a long spearcast, lie a plethora of religious sites. Melrose Abbey is here, and its Celtic predecessor, old Meuros. Dryburgh Abbey also, a druidical site of oak trees in a horseshoe bend of Tweed. Earl Haig, the general, is buried here, and possibly Michael Scott, a 12th-century genius with Eildon connections and a book of magic spells. Here are Bemersyde House, Monksford, Kirklands, and Holylee, the Roman camp of Newstead, the Masons of Melrose. Too many for coincidence, with the fairies in the centre exerting their pull and power.

So who were the fairies and what were they? Opinion varies between those who theorise about the supernatural and those who see a more practical answer. One supernatural theory claims that fairies are the spirits of the dead haunting the area where once they lived. Another theory proposes they could be creatures halfway between life and death, middle earth, a different dimension.

Perhaps they are a memory of older gods. "Cow lug" and

"Wag-at-the-wa" were fairy creatures from Bowden and Gattonside, touching on Eildon. Wag-at-the-wa was "a grizzlt-headed old man with yill-cap een, a mouth full of broken stumps, and one very long hooken front tooth" who laughed, joked and swung by his tail. That means a grizzle-headed man with one eye, a mouth full of broken teeth and one long, hooked front tooth. The Borderers kept him at arms-length by cutting a cross in their shepherds' crooks.

A child's tale? Nearby, remember, is the old Roman camp where archaeologists have found religious altars and where household gods, the Lares, were commonly honoured. Could this fairy be a distorted memory, given the Roman habit of settling time-served soldiers in Borderlands?

There is another possibility. The fairies might simply have been the people who were in the land before the current population. They were the original inhabitants. Many fairy tales speak of them as "people of peace", "good neighbours" or "seely folk", not as little winged creatures. They were much the same size as us, had faults and virtues like us, and enjoyed music and dancing.

Nothing wrong with that, nor with the fairies' closeness to nature: Border fairies ate bread that tasted of honey, ate silverweed and the tips of heather. They were fair-haired, dressed in green mantles inlaid with wildflowers and carried adder skin quivers containing bogreed arrows with poisoned flint heads. People still unearth these flint arrowheads throughout Scotland, known to our ancestors as elf shot and which people once believed possessed magical properties.

Once a year came the "Fairy Rade" when the good neighbours emerged in force. This raid or ride was an unchancy time when people or animals might be kidnapped, taken into a fairy hill and kept there. Women and baby boys were most vulnerable; the women needed for nurses and the boys captured in the hope they might grow into warriors to lead the fairies against the invaders. In their place were left "changelings", wrinkled old fairies who were a burden to their people.

Interestingly, we can see this process in more modern colonialism. The Bushmen of Southern Africa were small, used reed arrows were close to nature and attacked the cattle of invaders, both Boer and Bantu. Gaelic Highlanders raided the Lowlands for women, and did the Native Americans not kidnap women and children?

All were renowned for silent movement. Fairies were known as "the silent ones", again like the woodsmanship of the American Indians or African Bushmen. The fairies were frightened of iron, as Bronze Age or Stone Age people might be, but they used stone and other metals.

The rowan was a mystical tree to the Celts and effectively dealt with fairies, witches and the forces of evil. Even today there are newly built houses with rowans planted in the garden. In one street in the Borders town of Peebles, every tiny front garden came supplied with a rowan. And these are houses that date from the 1970s. Folk memory, purely decorative or a mixture of both?

Like Learmont (or Learmonth) himself, the tales are a blend of fact, fiction and wonder. About the middle of the 18th century, a womanising horse dealer named Dick Canonbie was preparing to sell his horses in Melrose when somebody warned him that an irate husband was searching for him. He left hurriedly, rounded the Eildons and stopped for the night at the western spur of the hills, known as Lucken Hare. It was now dark, and he was surprised when an old, white-bearded man approached and offered gold for his black horses. Dick agreed, sold the horses and took the money, ancient coins that were centuries out of date but still solid gold.

They met several times over the next year until Dick

became curious and asked where the elderly man lived, for this was a lonely place where the hill jutted into moorland, and shaggy heather merged with the straggled trees of Eildon. The old man agreed to tell Dick, warning that he would need all his courage.

Together they climbed up Lucken Hare until they came to a hidden cave. Inside was a vast stable of black horses and beside each horse lay a knight in black armour, asleep. By now, Dick was afraid. The old man showed him a carved oaken table, on top of which lay a hunting horn and a long sword. The old man spoke.

"Either draw the sword or blow the horn. Choose well, and you reign here as king: choose badly, and you forfeit your life. Trifle not with me for I am Thomas of Ercildoune."

Dick chose the horn, and the noise was deafening. All the knights sprang awake and only then did Dick draw the sword. The old man had vanished, but his voice sounded. "Woe to the coward that ever was born who did not draw the sword before he blew the horn."

Next morning Dick was found on the hillside, and he told his story before he died. Nobody has found that cave entrance again. Yet there was a strange new mark on the hill, like a galloping horse with a rider. A knight, perhaps, or a fair lady?

Were the Eildons home to supernatural beings, or just the old base for the Selgovae, the pre-Roman tribe who lived in the Borders? There are foundations of hundreds of ancient houses, the situation is excellent for defence, and there are springs for water, berries for food and at one time deer would roam free.

People have claimed to see an elderly man near the hills on summer nights, others have seen a black horse, and there has been a wild wind on Lucken Hare when the evening elsewhere is still.

One May Day, when we lived at Peebles, we visited Eildon

and heard a lone laverock, when the wind suddenly stopped. At that time, my younger daughter was five years old. She knew nothing of the legends but thought the place "spooky" and my wife, who can sense things, saw something moving on the eastern slopes. I do not believe in fairies but nor do I scoff at the tales.

PART FOUR
THE DEVIL'S SCOTLAND

INTRODUCTION

Scotland's enemies have sometimes equated Scottish soldiers with the Devil, probably because the Scots defeated them so often. Take the case of the English invasion of 1523, when they attacked Jedburgh. During the night, the local lads loosed 800 English horses, leaving the invaders unable to fight or flee. Unwilling to admit the Jeddart men had bested them once more, the English soldiers swore that the Devil was aiding the Scots and had released the horses.

In a more modern era, the First World War of 1914-1918, many German soldiers referred to the kilted Highlanders as the Ladies from Hell, which is perhaps a fitting nickname for men from Scotland, for this small country has a plethora of tales and legends in which the Devil figures.

Of course, Scots being what they are, they created a host of nicknames for the Devil, to avoid calling him by name – after all, it would never do to let the old codger know one was talking about him, and he could be listening at any street corner. For instance, in the Gaeltacht, the Gaelic-speaking area of Scotland, he could be called Domhnull Dubh, or Black Donald. In the Scots speaking area, he could be "Auld Hornie" or just "Hornie", "Auld Clootie", "Auld Nick", "the Queer Fellow", "the Earl of Hell", or "the Laird o' Yon Place". No doubt there were other, less printable names.

The Devil can pop up in a song, such as *The Deil's awa wi the Exciseman* and frequently in proverbs such as "deil a bodle," meaning nothing at all, or "deil mend ye if your leg was broken," meaning you are no good at the job you are trying. Many Scots will think that of politicians, particularly those based in Westminster. "The deil bides his time," is another, a warning that bad times are waiting for those who deserve them, or, "The deil gaes awa when he finds the door steekit (closed) against him," which is advice to resist temptation. Another, better known, is "the deil looks after his ain," in other words, evil people can prosper, although they will end in hell. Not as well known, perhaps is "the deil doesnae aye show his cloven cloots" – evil people can hide behind a charming exterior. There are many more.

The Devil features in many place names in Scotland too, sometimes with a story attached. For instance, there is the Deil's Barn Door, which is a col, a pass, between Auchenlone and Threehope Height in the Lowther Hills. One guide described this place as: "A small hollow, very much exposed to the high winds, which makes it very dangerous for travellers, more especially when snow is drifting." Better known is the Devil's Beef Tub, a dramatic hollow in the hills north of Moffat. There is no supernatural element here, but the Johnsons, one of the more energetic reiving families of south-west Scotland, were reputed to have hidden stolen cattle here.

In August 1685, at the height of the Killing Times when the forces of King James VII were persecuting Presbyterian Covenanters, one man named John Hunter was fleeing a party of dragoons. He tried to run up the steep sides of the Beef Tub, but Colonel Douglas's soldiers shot him. Colonel James Douglas was colonel of his majesty's regiment of foot guards, rather than the more notorious dragoons and was a noted persecutor of Covenanters. There is a small memorial here. Incidentally, the name "goons" for thugs is said to have derived from dragoons, who had an evil reputation for persecuting outlaws. William Wallace of *Braveheart* fame is also rumoured to have gathered his men here, which seems unlikely as it would be a natural trap.

There is also the Devil's Pulpit, in Finnich Glen near Kinnairn in Stirlingshire. According to legend, Auld Hornie did appear here and preached to a coven of witches and warlocks. More recently the Devilry of film in the personification of the series *Outlander* featured this 70-foot gorge, instigating a spate of tourists that imperilled the fragile environment, which is a new type of Devil, however well-meaning and welcome most might be. The water at the Pulpit runs red, but from red sandstone rather than blood, while the Pulpit itself is a mushroom-shaped rock. Visitors should take care as they descend the 78 Devil's Steps to this site of legend.

Druids are said to have met here, by the churning waters of the Finnich, while witches were reputed to have held satanic meetings, sacrificing people on the Pulpit. John Blackburn, the then-landowner built the twisting, narrow staircase in the early 19th century, and time has not been kind to them.

In Scotland, it is not always easy to see who the Devil is, for he can assume any form he desires, not always with the traditional cloven hooves and horns. More often, Old Nick would be a smooth-talking, handsome man who promises great things while delivering the exact opposite – a politician par excellence. On the odd occasion, he can arrive stark naked, which is taking a chance, given the Scottish climate, although perhaps a touch of frostbite in a delicate place might cure him of his hot temper. A cloud of Highland midges might do the same. The Devil could appear middle-aged, or elderly, a businessman or a labourer. It seems, though, that he cannot hide his cloven feet. If in doubt, check a stranger's feet and, if they are cloven, run.

Strangely, Auld Hornie does not seem to wear a kilt or any traditional Scottish dress, so he must be a visitor or an incomer to this fair nation.

Sometimes, it seems that the personage believed to be Auld Hornie is innocent of any Devilish devices. Before Caledonian MacBrayne's had the monopoly of ferries in the Hebrides, a company called Hutcheson ran a fleet of ships. One of their routes ran from West Loch Tarbert to Islay and a story, current at the time, said that when the first steam ferry arrived in Islay, the local folk crowded to witness this novel phenomenon. When one man saw the steward's pet monkey, he ran away, convinced that the Devil controlled the steamship.

Angus, that blessed region of fertile soil and frantic seas, seems to have been particularly favoured by the Devil if place names and traditions are any guides. One of the most notable devilish places thrusts off the coast just north of Arbroath. The Deil's Head is a rock formation, a sea stack, but in certain lights, the face of the Devil is quite clear although I could not find any legends attached. It is a splendid sight, though, when the sea runs high and the waves explode in spumes of spray and spindrift.

Further inland is Lundie where, in the 16th or 17th century, a shepherd was fond of playing his pipes, although the Kirk did not encourage such frivolity, as music was the Devil's device. The shepherd played most nights, sitting on a grassy knowe, looking over the countryside until one evening he heard the tune he had just played repeated to him. Perhaps thinking that somebody was joking with him, he played the song again, with the same result.

"Wha's there?" – who's there - he asked. When there was no reply, he stood up and looked all around, seeing nobody. He played again, to have the tune played back to him.

"Wha's there?" he asked again.

There was nobody. By now afraid, the shepherd played one more time, and again the unseen person echoed the same tune. Standing up, the shepherd smashed his pipes, knowing that only the Devil could play such a trick. He never again played a musical instrument.

The Devil also used Badenoch as a favoured stamping-ground. There used to be a defamatory saying that when God destroyed Sodom and Gomorrah, he forgot about Kingussie, the capital of Badenoch. Even if He had destroyed Kingussie, he would still have left badness, for people who were too wicked for Kingussie were said to live in neighbouring Newtonmore.

That might have been the reason the Devil liked to over-winter at Loch Gynack or Guinach, a little further up the hills. In the spring, he rose from the water, creating a huge wave. The wave poured across the nests of the black-headed gulls who lived at the edge of the loch. That amused his satanic majesty, for he was well aware that black-headed gulls are the angel's messengers. They hold the spirit of people who have done good deeds on earth and will soon be angels themselves. The blackness of the heads shows the few bad things they have done, and as soon as they have absolved their few sins, they will swap their feathers for angel's wings.

Not far downstream from the loch was a well, known only to the few who deserved to use it. According to local lore, drinking from that well gave immortality. I have looked for it, so far without success. Maybe next time!

THE DEVIL AND LORD REAY

Further north from Badenoch, the Devil was headmaster of a school for teaching his evil arts to the chiefs, lords and landlords of Scotland. One of his most accomplished students was Mackay, Lord Reay, who came from the very far north west. As soon as Lord Reay had passed his final exam, he knew he was as evil as the Devil, and proved it by his actions in turning Sutherland and Caithness into a battleground between the various clans.

Even the Devil was shocked by the carnage and suffering, so took Lord Reay aside and told him he'd have to quieten down his devilment. Lord Reay resented his ex-teacher trying to interfere in his domain and challenged him to a fight, a "square go" in later Scottish parlance. Sure of his hellish powers, the Devil agreed and Lord Reay beat him so severely that the Devil promised to leave Lord Reay to his own devices, throwing in a legion of demons to show there were no hard feelings.

That was all well and good, or well and bad, more accurately, but there is a drawback to having a host of demons as slaves. They need to be kept busy, or they get up to all kinds of mischief, as Lord Reay discovered. Any work Reay set them, they accomplished in no time, then demanded more, and more, and more again. Eventually, Lord Reay found a job for them. Sending them to the shore of his domains, he ordered them to make ropes of sand. They are still working.

A similar tale to that of Reay is told of a man called Donald Mackay, known as the Wizard of Reay. Hordes of demons beset him, all demanding work and sent them to the Bay of Tongue to make ropes out of the sand. Donald was a powerful wizard, who only had to wave his hand to summon snow, rain or hail from the sky.

There are other tales about Lord Reay and the Devil. Lord Reay may have been the first Lord Reay, a royalist soldier who took part in the Thirty Years' War, fighting under Gustavus Adolphus, and then fought in the wars that rocked Scotland, Ireland and England in the 1640s. At some time during his military service in Europe, he met the Devil – which makes sense given the devastation of the Thirty Years' War.

In this version of the story, the Devil had his school in Padua and invited Lord Reay to become a student. Lord Reay accepted at once and became an eager participant in every class. The Devil had a rule that, when each term ended, the students should scramble to leave, with the Devil claiming the soul of the last out of the great hall. When Lord Reay was last, he pointed to his shadow and said, "Deil tak the hindmost," whereupon the Devil grabbed the shadow and His Lordship escaped. Incensed at being tricked, the Devil chased Lord Reay from Padua to Sutherland, where they had their fight, and Lord Reay emerged as the victor.

According to this tale, the Devil and Lord Reay became good friends and often met on the frontier of Sutherland and Caithness, where the Devil entertained Lord Reay by playing the bagpipes. After all the excitement of wars and school, Lord Reay looked for further diversion, so decided to explore the Cave of Smoo, a spectacular series of caverns in north Sutherland. There are three interconnecting caves in Smoo, and his lordship took his dog with him. They explored the first cave thoroughly, but when they entered the second, the dog ran on ahead to the third. It came back a few moments later, howling in fear and with its hair singed off. Naturally, Lord Reay realised that the Devil was waiting for him, backed up with a hellish crowd of witches.

Checking the time, Lord Reay waited for a few moments before he approached the third cavern. He knew that down here and backed by his witches, the Devil would be stronger and able to defeat him. However, he also knew that it was nearly dawn and the Devil could not linger in this realm after the crow of the first cock. Sure enough, Lord Reay heard a cock and immediately the Devil and his cohorts knew they had to leave. Rather than fighting their way past Lord Reay, they blasted holes in the roof, and those holes are where the Smoo Burn now flows into the caves. Today the Smoo Caves are open for tourists, and a place worth visiting, although some tourists are less welcome as they leave their rubbish and human waste behind. With luck, Lord Reay will wreak his vengeance on these people.

Lord Reay was not the only Highlander to study at Padua, for the university there features in another tale that concerns the Devil and a Highland chief.

THE DEVIL AND CLANRANALD

CLAN DONALD WAS ONCE the dominant power in the Gaeltacht, the Gaelic speaking area of Scotland. They split into various regions, with MacDonald Clanranald possessing islands in both the Inner and Outer Hebrides as well as on the western mainland, with a clan seat at Castle Tioram in Moidart.

In 1670, with the civil wars finished and King Charles II on the throne, Donald Mhic Dhomhill, aged 46, became the chief of Clanranald. He was not the most pleasant of individuals. One of his more endearing hobbies was shooting at birds, animals and even people from the battlements of Castle Tioram, with his favourite musket, a beautifully crafted Spanish piece he called the Cuckoo. One misty day, Clanranald was on the ramparts when he thought he saw a man stealing his sheep. Aiming the Cuckoo, he fired a single shot that knocked the man into a well.

Seeing the man fall, some local men hurried over, pulled the man out and saw it was the Lad of the Wet Feet, one of Clanranald's servants. This servant had the job of walking through the heather in front of Clanranald, to ensure that his master's feet remained dry. When Clanranald heard the news, he merely shrugged, without making any comment. The life of a man, clansman or not, was not worth noticing.

That was not the only time that Clanranald showed a callous lack of concern. When one of his cooks stole his snuffbox, Clanranald ordered him to be hanged without any appeal. When Clanranald discovered somebody had stolen money, he suspected a maidservant, so tied her by the hair to a rock between the high and low tide marks and allowed her to drown. When the maid still refused to confess, Clanranald shifted the blame on to a ghillie and hanged him.

Naturally, such behaviour attracted the attention of the Devil, who sent a giant toad to Clanranald as an agent. When the toad came hopping to Clanranald and sat right beside him, there was no mistaking who and what it was. Taking it as a pet, Clanranald fed it well, so it blossomed into the most enormous toad anybody had ever seen and followed Clanranald like a faithful dog. People began referring to Clanranald as Black Donald of the Toad. Eventually, even Clanranald decided to part from his toad and threw it into the dungeon at Moidart. Boarding his galley, Clanranald sailed away, only to find that the toad had somehow escaped from its confinement and was swimming after him. As fast as his men rowed, the toad was always there, watching, with its head just above the water and its gaze never straying far from Clanranald's back.

Changing course, Clanranald steered for the island of Uist, but when he arrived, the toad was already waiting for him. Whatever he did, his familiar was there, watching. In 1686 Clanranald was on his island of Canna when he died, and the Devil came for him in person. Lying on his deathbed, Clanranald saw the clock strike midnight, heard a high-pitched whistle, and knew that the Devil was summoning him.

About to crawl from his bed, Clanranald felt his cousin, Ranald MacAilean Og, place a hand on his arm to hold him back.

When Ranald Og looked outside, he saw a tall creature with pointed ears standing on a prominent rock, roaring in anger and stamping its foot as it demanded that Clanranald approach it. Clanranald tried again to leave his bed, but Ranald had been a student at Padua University and knew sufficient of the black arts to fight back. All that night, Ranald and the Devil exchanged spells and counterspells, with the forces of evil clashing above the skies of Canna. With the first grey streak of dawn, a cock crowed, and the Devil knew he had lost. Screaming in frustrated rage, the Devil jumped into the sea as Clanranald left this mortal sphere and slid west to Tir nan Og, the land of eternal youth.

However, the Devil was not yet finished with the Clanranalds. With Donald dead, Allan Dearg became chief. In common with most of Clan Donald, Allan was a Jacobite so, when King James looked for men in 1715, he moved around the scattered lands and islands of Clanranald, calling out his clan. When he was in South Uist, a middle-aged speywife came to him to offer her blessing and a charm to keep him safe from harm. Allan accepted the charm, then recruited the speywife's teenage boy into his army. Naturally annoyed, the speywife pleaded with Allan to allow her son to stay behind, but the chief insisted. Clan chiefs had feudal power over their men, and it was common to call them to war with threats of eviction. The old idea that clansmen followed their chief out of love and devotion was not always accurate.

Immediately withdrawing her blessing, the speywife vowed that Allan would not return from the wars. Fishing inside her clothes, she brought out a battered silver sixpence. "Here is a crooked sixpence," she said to her son. "It has been seven times cursed. Let it avail you in battle against Allan Dearg to break my charm. Do this or you will have my curse upon your head."

The youth had little choice. He pocketed the coin and joined Allan Dearg's army that marched out to fight the usurper, King George. Perhaps Allan had heard the speywife say he would not return, or maybe he had a premonition of death for he ordered his men to burn Castle Tioram. He watched as flames destroyed his ancestral home, then marched south to King James's rendezvous.

There is no mystery about the outcome of that Jacobite rising. Bobbing Jock, the Earl of Mar, led the Jacobites against King George's regulars at Sheriffmuir. Although the Jacobites outnumbered King George's men, Red John of the Battles, John Campbell, 2nd Duke of Argyll, commanded the Hanoverian army. He was a veteran of many battles in Europe and more than a match for Mar. The two forces met at Sheriffmuir, near Stirling, where the right wing of each army destroyed the left wing of the other, but while Mar withdrew, Argyll remained static and won the day.

During the battle, in November 1715, Allan Dearg was said to be the only mounted Highlander on the Jacobite side, but although Red John's redcoats targeted him, the speywife's blessing kept him safe from harm. Watching from a distance, the speywife's son was in a dilemma. If he shot Allan, he might be hanged for treason against the Jacobites. If he did not shoot him, his mother's curse was waiting.

There was no competition. Loading his musket with the silver sixpence, the boy aimed at Allan and fired. He was either an exceptionally good shot or very lucky, for the missile hit Allan in the head. He fell off his horse, dead. As his clansmen gathered around, weeping. Glengarry had to call out to them in Gaelic, "Today for revenge, tomorrow for weeping," and they fell on the Hanoverians with their broadswords. After the battle, loyal clansmen carried Clanranald to Drummond Castle. Allan died and was buried in Innerpeffray chapel, where perhaps the Devil was satisfied with his revenge.

According to the story, well over 100 years later, somebody opened Allan's grave, to find his skull smashed, as though hit by a jagged object, such as a silver sixpence.

There is another angle to the tale that claims, rather than Castle Tioram that burned, it was Clanranald's castle at Ormacleit in South Uist. Clanranald had imported French builders, who took seven years to build the castle. Clanranald's family occupied it for seven years, and on the day of Clanranald's death, the chimney caught fire, and it burned to the ground. Or so the story claims.

THE DEVIL'S POINT

THE LAIRIG GHRU is one of the most significant passes in the Scottish Highlands, part of the 27-mile-long route from Aviemore to Braemar. It slices through the shadow of Scotland's second and third highest peaks, can harbour gales of up to 90 miles an hour, avalanches and blizzards. And yet it boasts some of the most beautiful hills in the country. Naturally, there are also stories and legends, with none stranger than that of Bod an Deamhain, often known as the Devil's Point although a more literal translation would be Penis of the Demon. According to legend, when Queen Victoria came along, she asked her ghillie, John Brown, what the name meant. He told her it was the Devil's Point, to avoid embarrassment although, as the queen had nine children, she would have seen the real thing often enough not to care. Never underestimate Good Queen Vic, I would say.

However, that is history. The Devil's Peak is slightly to the west of the pass, and the Gaelic name and the story date from at least the 17th century. According to the legend, a voice would wake local girls at night, repeatedly calling their names.

The call would start softly, gradually increasing in volume until the girl could not ignore it, but would rise to find out who the caller was. Another version of the tale claimed that the voice began as a whisper when the girls were young and grew stronger as the girls grew into women.

The voice was not threatening but soft and friendly. It continued all through the girls' childhood, but as soon as they became married women, it stopped. Only when the women fell pregnant did the calling start again. For some reason, the pregnant women were more susceptible to the call and followed the summons to climb Bod an Deamhain. On moonlit nights, the husbands and other relatives could see the women on the summit, slowly walking to the edge, and then they stepped off to plunge to their deaths on the rocks below. Even today, it is possible to hear the dying screams of the unfortunate women, or so it is said.

THE DEVIL AND THE BLACKSMITH

In Lochaber, there was a smith who was an expert in shoeing horses. He was so good that his fame spread right across Scotland and downwards to the other place. The Devil looked at his feet, decided they required new shoes and ventured into Scotland, found the smith in Badenoch and demanded a new set of Devil-shoes.

Annoyed at being awakened in the night, the smith fashioned the shoes, but when he attached them, he deliberately hammered the nails through the horn and into the Devil's flesh. Naturally, the Devil squealed and hopped around in agony. He shrieked for the smith to remove the nail and shoe him properly.

"Only if you make me a promise," the blacksmith said.

"Anything! Anything!" said the Devil, hopping around in agony.

"You must promise that, wherever a horseshoe hangs, no evil can enter, and that promise must endure for ever!"

"I promise!" Screamed the Devil, and that is why a horseshoe remains a charm against evil.

Strangely enough, I have also heard this story told about a blacksmith from Dingwall, so perhaps the Devil was foolish enough to try a second time.

THE GUDEMAN'S CROFT

There may still be some areas of land set aside for the Gudeman, somewhere in Scotland, although commercial farming has probably ended the custom. In old Scotland it was customary to leave a small corner of a field to lie waste, neither ploughed nor planted. This area was the Gudeman's Croft, the land left for the un-named, the Devil. Although the kirk tried to ban the practice, it continued well into the 19th century and possibly longer.

This land might be a neglected corner, or perhaps a knowe – a knoll that people once held sacred. The superstition, if it was that, held that if the farmer ever ploughed that area, there would be bad weather at least. So if you happen to see a corner of a field lying fallow or a small clump of trees on a knowe, you may well be looking at a place that holds a tradition that may be hundreds or thousands of years old. Sometimes, of course, the fairies could own the area, as in this story from the island of Coll. One day a crofter was tethering his pony on a fairy knowe, a sithean when a fairy popped his head up and told him to be more careful. The crofter had hammered his tether-peg into the ground on the sithean.

"You're letting the rain into our home," the little fellow said.

The crofter apologised and tethered his pony elsewhere.

The Gudeman's Croft or Devil's Croft could also be known as the Helliman Rig or Clouttie Croft. Corgarff in upland Grampian, near the Lecht pass and skiing centre, had two such places, both marked with a stone rampart to keep them secure. One was at Tornahaish, or Cheese Hillock, and the other at Delnadamph or Staghaugh, on the slope of Tornashaltic, or fire hillock. Fire hillock may hark back to the ancient days of fire festivals on Beltane.

According to tradition, the local folk sprinkled the Gudeman's Croft with milk on the First of April, to ensure no evil entered the house or the byre or barn. If the farmer inadvertently stepped into the sacred area, he would lose a tooth while, if his wife intruded, she would lose a stocking. A horse would shed a shoe and a cow a hoof, so it was best to keep clear.

THE DEIL AND THE TABLE

THIS NEXT TALE has versions in other parts of Scotland, including Rutland Barracks near Newtonmore, where the Wolf of Badenoch is the unfortunate man who plays cards with the Devil.

The House of the Binns in West Lothian is an atmospheric building that was home to Tam Dalyell, the head of the Scottish Army in the late 17th century.

General Tam Dalyell is undoubtedly a strange character in his own right and deserves a paragraph or three all to himself. His story will not only illustrate a half-forgotten slice of Scottish history but also gave meat to the later Devil legends. Tam Dalyell (1615-1685), began his military career while still in his teens, as many Scots still do. He fought for the Huguenots (Protestants) in France (one wonders if he faced the Three Musketeers), and travelled with the Scottish Army to Ulster to help protect the Protestant settlers from the indigenous Catholics.

Rising through the ranks to a Colonel, Dalyell returned to Scotland and marched south with the vastly outnumbered royal army that Cromwell defeated at Worcester. Imprisoned in the Tower of London, Dalyell managed to escape, which was no mean feat in itself. Fleeing from Cromwell's iron regime, Dalyell arrived in Russia, where he continued his military career, fighting, according to the stories, Poles, Turks and Tartars. He seemed quite settled in the East, even marrying a Russian woman. Nevertheless, on the accession of Charles II, he returned to the United Kingdom, bearing, according to legend, the unpleasant device of thumbscrews from Russia.

Dalyell, known as the Muscovite De'il (a play on the pronunciation of the name – De-yell – as the Devil was the De'il in Scotland), became General Dalyell, the Commander-in-Chief of the King's Army in Scotland. He raised five troops of horse and two regiments of infantry. Dalyell commanded the royal forces at the Battle of Rullion Green near Edinburgh when he defeated the Covenanters, extreme Presbyterians who fought for their religion. When the authorities jammed over a thousand prisoners in Greyfriars Kirkyard in Edinburgh, Dalyell added to his Muscovite nickname with another, Bluidy Tam.

Dalyell was also involved in the later Killing Times when Royal forces put down another Covenanter rising. However, it was not until after he died that the ghosts walked at his house of the Binns. There are three main stories. The first states that a spectre on a white horse gallops towards the Binns at night, presumably Bluidy Tam himself. The second says that Dalyell's cavalry boots march around the house at night. The third is where the Devil meets the De'il, and furniture goes flying.

According to the legend, Dalyell and the Devil used to play cards on a particular marble-topped table. The Devil usually won, probably because he was a cheating hound, but Dalyell had tricks of his own and rearranged the room, so he had a mirror behind the Devil. Now he could see the Devil's cards, Dalyell won trick after trick until Auld Hornie realised what was happening. Lifting the table, he kicked it at Dalyell with a mouthful of Devilish oaths. Dalyell ducked, and the table flew outside the house to land in the Sergeant's Pond in the grounds, where it sank below the surface and vanished. The pond is also known as the Colonel's Pond and apparently, when Dalyell raised the Scots Greys cavalry regiment, the horses drank there.

As time passed, people forgot where the table was. Not until the drought-stricken summer of 1878 was the table found again. It now sits in the entrance hall of the Binns, where any visitor can examine it. And it is worth examining, with its white marble top and floral design. It's a pity that the precious stones are now missing, but not surprising given the table's adventures. The table is presumed to be Mughal, so made in India, and must have seen some travelling even before Dalyell carried it to Scotland. However, in one corner, there is a definite mark in the shape of the Devil's hoof to prove the story of Old Nick kicking the table through the window.

Of course, it is possible that the whole story was invented after somebody recovered the table!

There are other interesting facts about Dalyell and the Binns. He built the west wing, which gives the house a U or horseshoe shape, and the Devil is scared of horseshoes. Another legend says that, on one occasion, Dalyell and the Devil had a heated argument and the Devil threatened to blow the building down. When Dalyell replied he would build strong walls, the Devil said no walls would be sufficiently strong to withstand him, so Dalyell added stout turrets to nail the house down. The turrets are still there, holding down the Binns.

When Dalyell died in his house in the Canongate, now part of Edinburgh, he was buried at Abercorn. His boots were reversed and hung from the saddle of his horse, as was traditional. After the burial, Dalyell's son John fell heir to the boots and carried them to his home in Fife. He soon regretted that, as the boots marched around the house at night. They also had the unique skill of boiling water without a fire; simply pour cold water inside the boots, and it would come to the boil. Dalyell may have been dead, but he still visited the Binns, riding a white horse past the Black Lodge, the old road between South Queensferry and Bo'ness and into the estate by the bridge over the Errack Burn. Perhaps he still does.

THE DEVIL'S BROOD

Some families are born to badness. It seems to run through the blood, and in the late 17th and early 18th centuries, the Douglases of Drumlanrig acquired the local name of the Devil's Brood. William, the First Duke of Queensberry and Marquis of Dumfriesshire was also the Lord High Treasurer and President of the Council. Yet people disliked Drumlanrig, possibly because of his reputation as a moneylender, the profits of which helped finance his utterly entrancing Castle of Drumlanrig. This gentleman was said to tyrannise his wife by refusing her money, he argued with his son and fought with his sister-in-law. Drumlanrig's sister, Lady Margaret Jardine, was an independently wealthy woman, yet she still ferried travellers across the River Annan, charging a halfpenny for the trip.

According to legend, when the Duke died in 1695, a Scottish shipmaster was trading in Sicily and saw a coach-and-six driving straight into the mouth of Mount Etna. The volcano was erupting at the time, and a formidable voice roared: "Make way for the Duke of Drumlanrig!"

The story may not be strictly accurate, but gives an idea of the regard in which the Scots people held the duke. He died in Queensberry House in Edinburgh, a building that held infamy in later years. The Duke's family were not lucky, with his daughter, Anne, Countess of Wemyss, burning to death in a tragic accident in February 1700 while his son earned everlasting infamy as the Union Duke. He was one of the men who signed the Treaty of Union in 1707, accepting payment of £12,325 from the London parliament. The southern authorities also rewarded him with the titles of Duke of Dover, Marquis of Beverley and Baron Ripon. In Scotland, he was detested as a traitor and, chased out of Edinburgh, while the good neighbours of Edinburgh and the Canongate stoned Queensberry House.

While the Union Duke was appending his signature to the treaty, his elder son, James, Earl of Drumlanrig, was busily killing and roasting a young servant in Queensberry House. The good citizens of Edinburgh nodded sagely and told each other that his family troubles were God's judgement on him for signing the Union. The young servant laddie might have wondered why he was the ultimate victim, though.

While the Union Duke's elder son was munching his way through the household staff, his younger son succeeded to the title and married Catharine Hyde, whose father was the Earl of Clarendon, an English nobleman. Again the curse struck for she proved to be an extremely unpleasant woman subject to such a violent temper that her husband had to restrain her in a straitjacket. Although they occasionally lived in Queensberry House, Catharine did not like Scotland or the Scots and constantly ridiculed them, dressing as a peasant and mocking Scottish pretentiousness and accents. Their son broke off his engagement to one woman to marry another and eventually committed suicide, an act that surprised nobody in Scotland.

Sir Robert Grierson of Lagg was another friend of the

Devil. During the Killing Times of the 1670s and 1680s, he had been a noted persecutor of Covenanters. When he died in 1733, a sudden storm encompassed a ship on the Solway Firth. The wind rose, black clouds engulfed the vessel, and then a sudden shaft of moonlight revealed a black coach, drawn by six black horses.

"Whither bound?" asked the shipmaster.

"To tryst with Lagg, from Hell."

Such was the power of the Devil in old Scotland, when everybody had firm opinions on religion and believed their opponents were agents of evil.

PART FIVE
STRANGE TALES AND PEOPLE

THE LADY WHO WAS BURIED THREE TIMES

Most people are buried only once, usually after they are dead. However, that was not the case with the Lady Grange, who managed to get herself interred three times, once when alive, and twice after she died.

Most accounts name her as Rachel Chiesley, some call her Ann, although none argue about her disposition. Even before she married, Rachel Chiesley was a quick-tempered, hard-drinking supporter of the House of Hanover, the sort of woman one would cross the road to avoid. When she married James Erskine, Lord Grange, people shook their heads, knowing there would be fireworks in that household, even though Rachel was an undoubted beauty.

It was the early 18th century, and two factions faced each other across a bitter divide. On one side were the Jacobites, who supported the autocratic and Roman Catholic House of Stuart. On the other were the Hanoverians, who wished the Germanic Georges of the Protestant House of Hanover to keep their plump bottoms on the throne of the United Kingdom. If politics and religion divided the kingdom, then they also split the house of Grange, for James Erskine was as ardent a Jacobite as Rachel was a Hanoverian. Not only did Lord Grange follow the Stuarts, but he also had strong family connections, being the brother of the Earl of Mar, that infamous Bobbing Jock who had raised the Stuart Standard on the Braes of Mar in the rising that ended in failure at the bloody battle of Sheriffmuir.

Presumably, the marriage between Lord Grange and Rachel Chiesley (one of several spellings of the name) was a union of love, or perhaps lust, for in all other ways they seem mismatched. By the 1730s, if not before, Lord Grange was a central figure in the Jacobite intrigues that bubbled under the surface of the Scottish nation. That was the period of Jacobite secret toasts when they were supposed to be pledging loyalty to the crown. As they were raised, the wine glasses were passed over a vessel containing water, such as a finger bowl, to symbolise "the king over the water" – the exiled Stuarts. It was the period of plans and schemes, of Highland chiefs visiting quiet rendezvous in the Lowlands, of claymores hidden in heather-thatch and contacts made with foreign governments for landings of trained soldiers and shipments of gold. It was also the period when the Black Watch, the Hanoverians' first regular Highland regiment, began to patrol the glens to maintain order, and the British government built new barracks and roads to pacify the Gaeltacht.

The times were undoubtedly exciting, but such activities also diverted attention from other matters, for in 1707 Scotland had been dragged into a parliamentary Union with England and Wales, probably by bribery, corruption and threats of economic and military force. Although the vast majority of Scotland's population were wildly opposed to the Union, the few at the top accepted the new titles, pocketed the money and tried to avoid the approbrium of their countrymen. Now Scotland was paying the price as trade along the east coast stagnated, Edinburgh was like a wasteland as the elite drained down to London and poverty stalked the towns. Men including Lord Grange hoped that a return to the Stuart dynasty might bring some prosperity to a sadly struggling country.

To achieve that, he had to meet men of similar mind and avoid his wife, for Rachel's temper was notorious and seems to have been a family trait. Rachel's father, John Chiesley of Dalry had possessed an equally vicious temper as well as an ability to harbour a grudge for years. John Chiesley married a lady named Margaret Nicholson, and despite having 10 children together, he was not happy with his wife. When Margaret took him to court, the judge, George Lockhart of Carnwath, Lord President of the Court of Session, found in her favour and said that Chiesley should pay her 1,700 merks. Chiesley never forgave Lockhart for that judgement.

In late 1688, Chiesley was in London, drinking with an advocate named Sir James Stuart, or Stewart, and mentioned that he was "determined to go to Scotland before Candlemas and kill the President". Stuart shook his head gravely and said: "The very imagination of such a thing is a sin before God."

"Let God and me alone," Chiesley said. "We have many things to reckon betwixt us, and we will reckon this, too."

It was on Sunday, 31 March 1689, when the dislike between the Protestant forces of William of Orange and the Catholic forces of King James VII erupted into civil war, that Chiesley seized his opportunity for revenge. Edinburgh was in turmoil, with the Williamite forces besieging King James' garrison in the castle, but life still carried on in the streets and wynds beneath. Lockhart was returning from church to his home in either Mauchline Close or, more likely, Old Bank Close when Chiesley crept up out of the dark and shot him in the back. A group of men, possibly members of Lockhart's family and including Lord Castlehill and Daniel Lockhart, grabbed Chiesley and took Lockhart home. Lady Lockhart was in bed, heard the pistol shot and ran into the street in her nightdress. While Lockhart died that same night, the men hustled Chiesley to the authorities.

Chiesley immediately admitted the murder. "I am not wont to do things by halves," he said. "And now I have taught the president how to do justice."

Nevertheless, the authorities still tortured him to see if he had acted alone or had accomplices. When they were satisfied he was alone, he was tried and sentenced to death. The authorities added some refinements to the execution. They fastened Chiesley to a hurdle, dragged him to the Mercat Cross, tied his pistol around his neck and hanged him. His right hand was also chopped off and attached to the West Port, the western gateway into Edinburgh. Finally, the authorities ordered that Chiesley's corpse should be chained and displayed at the Gallow Lee, halfway between Edinburgh and Leith, until it rotted away.

So much for justice tinged with mercy. The hangman carried out the execution as required, and hoisted Chiesley's body on the gallows at Gallow Lee. However, it had hardly decorated the gallows when it vanished. The rumour in Edinburgh was that his friends had stolen it for a secret and more honourable burial, but nobody knew for sure. Naturally, Chiesley's ghost remained, haunting his old manor house of Dalry so that servants avoided the back kitchen. They believed the old wives' tale that Chiesley had been secreted back to his house and buried under the hearth.

Then, about 100 years later, a workman was renovating the ancient garden wall. There was a slight recess, with a stone seat. The workman shifted the seat and jumped back in alarm. He had found a human skeleton, with the right hand missing. However, an alternative story in *Traditions of Edinburgh* by

Robert Chambers says the skeleton was found underneath a hearthstone in Dalry Park, with the pistol around the neck.

With such a father, we may excuse Rachel for her temper. Perhaps she was mentally deranged. She certainly knew that her husband was a Jacobite. According to one story, she was rummaging through her husband's chest of drawers and found a document that named him alongside Sir Alexander MacDonald of Sleat, Fraser of Lovat and Norman MacLeod of Dunvegan. The legend claimed that all these men were in a Jacobite plot to restore the Stuarts to the British throne.

By that time, Rachel had already been married for 20 years and had nine children, while Lord Grange had been Lord Justice Clerk since 1710. Perhaps Rachel's "wild beauty" had been a factor in her pre-marital pregnancy, yet she was apparently still able to squeeze under a sofa when Lord Grange and his cronies gathered in his house in Niddry's Wynd. She listened to their plotting, but either some dust got up her nose, and she sneezed, or she just had plain bad luck, for the Jacobites discovered her. From then on, life became unpleasant for Rachel, Lady Grange. Within seconds, the conspirators pounced on the unfortunate lady, wrapped a blindfold around her eyes, tied her securely and debated what they should do.

With the fate of the kingdom at stake, they could not allow Rachel to roam free in the capital city, yet Lord Grange balked at killing his wife, so the Jacobites decided to place her somewhere safe. On 22 January 1732, MacDonald of Morar and Roderick MacLeod of Berneray, two Highland gentlemen, entered Edinburgh with a body of their men. They grabbed Rachel, who shrieked and struggled, but against half a dozen wiry Highlanders had little chance. Gagging her, they threw her into a sedan chair and carried her out of Edinburgh. Opening the sedan chair, they threw Lady Grange face down over a horse and rode through the night to Falkirk, then up to the Highlands. Here, the MacGregors, Children of the Mist, took her to the Monach Islands and over the sea to Skye.

To cover her disappearance, Lord Grange told everybody his wife had suddenly died, and there was false grief as a weighted coffin was carried through the streets and buried in St Cuthbert's Churchyard. Nobody checked the body, for who would doubt the word of a gentleman and a lord? So that was Rachel's first burial, while the MacGregors and others were smuggling her to Idrigill on the Isle of Skye.

After the bustle and sophistication of Edinburgh, living in confinement in Skye must have been an ordeal for Lady Grange. At the same time, Rachel's explosive temper would make her jailers' life equally unpleasant. However, Rachel wrote a note explaining her predicament and smuggled it to her relatives in a skein of wool, then sat back waiting for deliverance from her nest of Jacobites. Nothing happened, although her captors may have got wind of her endeavours for they shoved her on board a small boat and transported her to the even more remote Island of Heisker on the west coast of North Uist. Here, with only Gaelic-speaking Jacobites for companionship and the wild Atlantic crashing all around, Rachel must have regretted getting involved in politics. After two years on Heisker, her jailers moved her again, even farther away, to St Kilda, the island on the edge of the world, where the inhabitants scarcely saw a visitor, lived mainly on birds' eggs and knew nothing of Jacobites or Hanoverians. Life itself was struggle enough without indulging in dynastic politics.

For seven years, Rachel, Lady Grange remained on lonely St Kilda, and only when talk of rescue reached MacLeod of Dunvegan, who owned that outpost of Scotland, did he think of moving her. According to the story, she was taken first to Assynt on the west coast of the Scottish mainland, and then back to Skye. Rather than live in a house, Rachel resided in a cave near the Point of Idrigill. Perhaps it was not surprising that her sanity slipped away, which allowed her jailers to relax her confinement, so she had a measure of freedom. Not long after, she was in a cottage in Vaternish, where she died, never having seen Edinburgh again.

For some reason, Rachel's captors held another mock burial. Filling a coffin with peat, they solemnly interred it at Duirnish. In the meantime, Rachel's body was carried to Trumpan Churchyard, also in Skye, for its third and final burial where there is a simple grey slab to commemorate her tragic last few years.

There are other versions of the story, of course. It is equally possible that Rachel found out that her husband was conducting an affair with Fanny Lindsay, who ran a coffee house in Edinburgh. In response, Rachel, then over 50 years old, threatened to run naked around the streets of Edinburgh or commit suicide. The former choice might have enlivened the city, which was not at its best in 1730, while the latter might have relieved Lord Grange of his troublesome wife. However, Rachel did neither. Instead, she slept with a cut-throat razor under her pillow and repeatedly mentioned her murderous father, no doubt hoping to intimidate Lord Grange. It was evident that there was no longer love in the marriage, and on 27 July 1730, the couple agreed on a formal separation. That might have suited his lordship, but Rachel still nursed her wrath.

Whenever Lord Grange appeared in the streets of Edinburgh, Rachel was there, shouting and screaming at him, pointing an accusing finger and calling him every unpleasant name she could bring to mind. She even yelled at him inside the church and did not reserve all her vituperation for her husband, for on at least one occasion she abused one of her sons until he took refuge in a tavern, refusing to emerge until she had gone. Rachel also planted herself outside Lord Grange's house in Niddry's Wynd, swearing at the top of her voice, which was not the behaviour expected from a lady of her standing. Nevertheless, it was not until 1732, when Rachel booked a seat on a London-bound stagecoach that Lord Grange acted. Apprehensive that his estranged wife might reveal his covert support for the Stuart cause, Lord Grange arranged her kidnapping, and the rest is history.

What is interesting is the lack of support for Rachel. When she suddenly disappeared, none of her children questioned her sudden death; perhaps Rachel's vicious temper had killed any love they once had. Lord Grange was not only old-fashioned in his desire to return to the Stuart dynasty, but he also opposed laws that repealed witchcraft, so he was out of mainstream thinking. As soon as Rachel was officially dead and three times buried, Lord Grange married his long-time lover, Fanny Lindsay. His house disappeared when city improvements swept away Niddry's Wynd, and the South Bridge was erected instead. We will allow Dr Johnson to have the last word on the kidnapping of Lady Grange in St Kilda: "if Macleod had let it be known that he had such a place for naughty ladies, he might make it a very profitable island."

GHOST TRAIN OF DAVA

When we lived in Moray, one of our favourite places was Dava Moor. It is a large tract of moorland, bisected by a couple of minor roads, and harbours Lochindorb, one of the most romantic of Scottish castles, that sits on an island in a loch of the same name. The castle was a home of Alasdair Stewart, the notorious Wolf of Badenoch, whom people suspected of dabbling in the black arts, and perhaps it is his memory that gives the moor its slightly sinister air.

Not in high summer, when there is nowhere more pleasant than the Dava Way footpath that stretches from Forres to Grantown-on-Spey. But the onset of winter alters everything. On a black night in December, with a smirr of snow in the air and strange sounds in the distant moor, Dava can convey a different atmosphere entirely.

It was on just such a night in 1917 when a gentleman named John Macdonald was walking home. He was following a track beside the railway line that is now the Dava Way, no doubt slipping on the hard-frozen snow as he walked between Dunphail and Dava. He heard the sound first and then saw something that remained with him for the rest of his life as a locomotive appeared in the sky, pulling four trucks as it plunged down in a blaze of light and powered past Macdonald. He saw the train, and he saw the smoke and steam from its funnel, grey-white against the dark sky.

Now, a winter night can be deceptive. I have driven that road a hundred times in all seasons, and I know that lights can play tricks on a tired mind. However, John Macdonald was not the only man to see that train that night, for the farmer at Kerrow, a few miles away, also witnessed the phenomenon.

What was it? What caused the sighting and why? There are many questions and very few answers. There do not seem to have been any train crashes on this stretch of line, except for one incident in the late 1870s when a cattle train caught fire at Dava and about 40 animals died in the blaze.

Nevertheless, there were other sightings of the phantom train. On 25 October 1919, John Macdonald saw it again. After an evening at Berryburn croft, beyond Dunphail, Macdonald was returning home on his bicycle with a full moon glossing the moor and the dying heather in the hills beyond. He was coming to Achnolachan when a startlingly bright light dazzled him, and he fell from his bicycle. Shaken, but unhurt, Macdonald stared at the light, which soon faded away. He came back the next day, to find nothing unusual on the line. However, other people, including a Mr Calder, a local railwayman, had witnessed the same phenomenon, without anybody knowing the reason. The Macdonald clan seem to have been tuned in to whatever spiritual aspect the train had, for in 1949, 30 years later, Mrs Macdonald, John's mother, was near Bogney when she heard a train. Knowing there were no trains scheduled, she ignored the sound, until she looked behind her and saw the ghost train steaming along with its firebox gleaming and nobody on the footplate. Naturally startled, Mrs

Macdonald fled away from the line and tripped and fell as the ghostly train roared past, floating two feet above the railway.

The railway has now gone, with the cuts of the 1960s removing the line, as it did so many others. Perhaps the ghostly train has also gone, but with supernatural apparitions, one can never tell.

THE TAY BRIDGE GHOST

The fall of the Tay Bridge at Dundee was one of the worst transport disasters of the 19th century. A bridge collapsing at any time is terrible, but a bridge collapsing when a passenger train is passing over is shocking.

The Tay Bridge disaster was even worse as there were no survivors. Seventy-five people – every passenger plus the driver – died when the train plunged into the dark waters of the River Tay at quarter past seven on 28 December 1879. Yet that did not seem to be the end of the story. Skilful engineers erected a new bridge on the site of the old, and on the anniversary of the tragedy, people travelling across the Tay began to have strange experiences.

There was the young male traveller for instance, who boarded the train in Fife, bound for Dundee and points north. He realised that he was the only person in his compartment except for one silent elderly man in clothes that were at least a decade out of fashion. As they neared the new Tay Bridge, the elderly man began to look nervous, and as they passed above the dark waters of the river, the man's face altered to a look of horror. The young man tried to speak, but rather than answering, the elderly man slowly disappeared.

Was this a memory of a passenger on that fated train? Or was the young man affected by the knowledge of the tragedy? After all, it's not hidden as the stumps of the old bridge can clearly be seen beside the new, thrusting out of the water like the tombstones of the lost passengers.

There are other stories of a ghost train that can be seen on the anniversary of the disaster, steaming on the site of the old bridge, and the sound of screaming passengers as the train plunges into the bitter water. Although I lived in Dundee for 10 years, I never met anybody who admitted personal experience of this ghostly train.

HAUNTED MONTROSE AIRFIELD

Montrose, about halfway up the East Coast of Scotland, is one of the most historic towns in the country. From Norse raids to English armies, smugglers and fishermen, trade with the Baltic and North America and a plethora of historical figures, Montrose has seen it all. Yet arguably the most famous ghost is an Irish flier from the early 20th century.

The airfield at Montrose was one of the oldest in the world and, in February 1913, Number 2 Squadron, Royal Flying Corps, the predecessor of the Royal Air Force, landed here as its base. The RFC intended Montrose as a training airfield, which is said to make it the oldest training base in the United Kingdom.

One of the early fliers was Lieutenant Desmond Arthur from County Clare, Ireland, who tragically died in an accident at Montrose Airfield on 27 May 1913. His ghost was walking as lately as 2018. Witnesses report seeing a young man dressed in flying gear that was current before the First World War, so it was not a modern flier seen in the half-light. Arthur's ghost appears in various places but most often coming out from a mist and walking through a solid wall.

Twenty-eight-year-old Lieutenant Arthur was flying a BE2 aircraft when the upper wing broke, and the machine plunged 2,000 feet out of the sky. At that early period, pilots did not wear parachutes, so would have little chance of survival. Arthur died immediately, with every bone in his body broken, and the aircraft landed some 160 yards away. That tragedy was the first RFC death at Montrose so it must have shocked the eager young flying men.

When the RFC investigated the accident, they discovered that the fitters had not correctly completed a repair to the upper wing of the biplane, causing the crash. However, that was not the end of the story, for although the RFC buried Arthur at the nearby Sleepyhillock Cemetery, he seemed determined not to leave the airfield. He returned within a few years, checking on his companions as war raged across the world and the infant RFC expanded into the much larger RAF. By 1915, the airfield at Montrose was hectic, with the barracks crammed with officers and keen young men hoping to do their part in defeating Kaiser Bill. The following year, Lieutenant Arthur rejoined them. At that time, another inquiry into the crash blamed Arthur for stunt flying. Perhaps he was returning to clear his name.

A Major Cyril Foggin (I have also seen the name as Foggit) was the first recorded RFC officer to meet the deceased lieutenant. Others soon followed until Arthur became an accepted, if not always welcome, member of the airfield, with most sightings occurring at the old Mess of No 2 Squadron. There are stories of sentries retreating at speed from the ghost, and the more nervous officers requesting transfers away from Montrose.

More than that, for in the late 1930s, as Hitler's War

loomed on the horizon, Arthur seemed to cast a helpful blanket over the men training and flying from Montrose.

He remained in place as the world exploded into war in 1939, occasionally joined by ghostly companions. The German Luftwaffe opened the war with a raid on the Firth of Forth, which put Scotland right in the front line. By 1940, the Battle of Britain was in full swing, and German raids were a daily occurrence so Scottish-based aircraft were constantly on guard. On one occasion, the pilot of a Hurricane was quartering the sky for a Heinkel bomber when an ancient biplane caught his attention. Was Lieutenant Arthur trying to help? Two years later, after another crash, a second ghost appeared, possibly the recently dead man, but who was the ghost in a white flight suit that people saw until the airfield ceased operations in the 1950s?

Were these ghosts different fliers? Or was it Lieutenant Arthur returning to his old haunts? To close this piece, I will add that Arthur had a romantic side, for when his body was recovered, he had the photograph of a girl in his pocket. Winsom Ropner was barely a teenager, yet Arthur had visited her parents in Hartlepool, and the two were more than friends, so much so that Arthur left her a great deal of money in his will. On a happy note, Winsom married in 1918, naming her first son Desmond, after Arthur.

MACGREGOR AND THE COLONY THAT NEVER WAS

STRANGELY, despite my wandering across this frustrating country of Scotland, I have only once known anybody with the surname MacGregor. He was an extreme Scottish Nationalist – and no shame at all in that – except he took his extremism a little far. He was not born with the name MacGregor but with the much more prosaic one of Brown. But, clearly, in his mind, Brown was not sufficiently Scottish, so he changed it to MacGregor, and in so doing, joined one of the most beleaguered and exciting of all the Scottish clans, at least in name.

The MacGregors, the so-called Children of the Mist, have been extensively written about, and this is not the place to add more. However, sufficient to say that they were a clan with a history of outlawry, raiding and general wildness that spanned several centuries. Thanks to Sir Walter Scott, Rob Roy MacGregor is arguably the best known, and Gregor MacGregor is barely known at all, which makes him all the more interesting.

In 1811, Gregor MacGregor was a soldier in the Black Watch, the 42nd Regiment of Foot when South American revolutionaries sailed to Britain to recruit soldiers for their cause. Gregor signed up, to find Venezuela in the New World crawling with Gaelic-speaking Highlanders in this ugly war against the colonial power of Spain.

Gregor must have inherited the military skills of his ancestors for he quickly made himself at home in the polyglot revolutionary army, and rose through the ranks in a manner that would have been unthinkable in class-conscious Britain. He became a commissioned officer, then a General of Cavalry, and a General of Brigade, and finally, a General of Division. Simón Bolívar awarded him the Order of Liberators and allowed him the hand of his cousin, Doña Josefa Aristeguieta y Lovera.

Gregor was anything but a parade-ground soldier. He fought in the tropical forests and the mountains, combining cavalry with infantry, defeating superior numbers of trained Spanish forces, but also losing men in failed campaigns.

With Venezuela freed, Gregor began operations in Central America, on the disease-ridden Mosquito Coast. Here, he found traces of a decades-old former British colony and became friendly with a local chief. Perhaps Gregor had been planning some major coup for a long time, or maybe the idea came to him on the Mosquito Coast, but he changed from freedom fighter and successful soldier to one of the greatest confidence tricksters the world has ever known. Some people can scam for a few pounds or even a few million pounds, others can sell a dodgy car or house, but only a MacGregor could invent an entire country and fool kings and commoners into believing it existed.

Once Gregor had the idea, he wasted no time into putting things in practice. Persuading the elderly local chief into signing a spurious document to cede a vast tract of land, Gregor folded the manuscript and took the first ship back to Britain. He may have left Scotland as a plain soldier of the 42nd Foot, but he arrived back as His Serene Highness, Gregor I, Prince of Poyais, with the beautiful Doña Josefa as his princess. Years had passed since Gregor sailed to the west, and now King George IV's royal posterior was planted on the throne of the United Kingdom. Gregor presented himself at the Court of St James, and with so many new countries springing up all across the Americas, it is perhaps not surprising that the public accepted Gregor as the genuine article. All it needed was a brass neck, a touch of arrogance and the blood of Clan Gregor. After all, the MacGregor motto is *Royal is my Race,* and they claim blood older and more native to Britain than any upstart Hanoverian princeling.

Gregor did not skimp on details. He invented a knightly order, the Illustrious Order of the Green Cross and used British printing presses to produce banknotes of the imaginary Kingdom of Poyais. Gregor also had his chargé d'affaires, one William Richardson, create marketing brochures of his marvellous kingdom. People who had never thought about the Mosquito Coast and certainly had never known about Poyais were soon discussing this fantastic country as if they knew it well. They examined illustrations of Poyais' capital city with its clean, broad streets, its bridges across a sparkling river and its magnificent public buildings. They also spoke of its gold and its silver mines, its jewels and excellent timber. Gregor had laid it on with a shovel, using all the charm and duplicity that centuries of anti-MacGregor oppression had taught him.

One of his advertisements appeared in the *Caledonian Mercury* of 25 April 1822:

North America
> A Baronial Estate for Sale in the Territory of Poyais
> The Territory of Poyais is situated in the Bay of Honduras. It is remarkable for its salubrity of climate, and

for richness and productiveness of soil. Edwards in his History of the West Indies (last edition), Long in his History of Jamaica; Captain Wright, (who being many years senior naval officer in the Bay of Honduras, had every opportunity of being well acquainted with the country), in his Memoir of the Mosquito Territory; and Henderson, in his account of the British Settlement of Honduras – all speak in the highest terms of "this delightful and most valuable country", and of its great capabilities, both commercial and agricultural.

Besides these advantages, the purchaser may acquire many valuable privileges.

The particulars may be learned, and every Information obtained, by application personally, or by letter, (post paid) addressed to the Agent, at this office.

Lands in the above territory are now on sale in the following quantities, as formerly advertised, Viz –

A section of 640 acres............£64

Half, 320 acres....................£32

Quarter, 160 acres................£16

Eighth, 80 acres..................£8

Sixteenth, 40 acres...............£4

Being at the rate of two shillings per acre, but in a few weeks the price will be two shillings and sixpence per acre and a still further advance will take place soon thereafter.

POYAIS LAND OFFICE, 12 ROYAL EXCHANGE,
Edinburgh, April 7th 1822.

All well and good, but what was the point of this breathtaking lie?

Money.

Within days, Gregor had borrowed £200,000, with the assets of his kingdom as security. That was only the start. With London in his pocket and hundreds of thousands of pounds in his bank account, Gregor next journeyed to Edinburgh. Here he sold land in his kingdom at the bargain price of four shillings – 20 pence – an acre. Men who could never dream of owning property in their native land purchased vast tracts of Poyais, exchanging their Scottish money for the Bank of Poyais notes. Gregor encouraged them, pocketed their gold and no doubt whistled a merry ditty.

In time, ships full of hopeful emigrants sailed from Leith to the tropical paradise of Poyais. They expected to find a beautiful city and acres of fertile land. Instead, they saw a tropical wilderness, while a hurricane battered their ships.

Nevertheless, the settlers possessed native pluck and tried to make the best of things. They built huts, searched for help, caught malaria and died by the score. When news of the colonists' plight reached British Honduras, further along the coast, the authorities sent ships to rescue the survivors. Naturally, news of the disaster reached Britain, where Gregor said the British government's agent in British Honduras, a Scotsman named John Young, was launching a personal attack on him.

Gregor laughed off such scurrilous nonsense as false news.

Having said his piece and made his money, Gregor promptly vacated Scotland and shipped across to France, where he repeated the whole sorry business, with equal success. However, the sun was setting on the Court of Gregor. He visited London and found himself jailed, talked his way to freedom, returned to Paris, was incarcerated again and eventually found his way to Venezuela, where he spent the rest of his life.

Some Scottish tales are strange indeed, but none can outstrange Clan Gregor.

THE ABBEY VAMPIRE

There is nowhere quite like the Scottish Borders. At one time it was one of the most bitterly contested pieces of land in the world, and the atmosphere of tension can still be felt by those capable of sensing such things. It was here that the Roman Empire ended, for the Borders are only a few score miles north of Hadrian's Wall, the only stretch of land in a frontier some thousands of miles long where the Romans felt it necessary to build a wall of solid stone. On these hills, fields and gentle valleys, Picts and Dalriadic Scots, Angles and Britons fought as frontiers surged back and forth. King Arthur may have lived here, and in later times William Wallace, the Black Douglas, the Dark Knight of Liddesdale, the Bold Buccleuch and Black Archibald the Grim all left their mark. It is undoubtedly one of the most storied areas of the world, yet few people know about the vampire of Melrose Abbey.

Melrose is one of the jewels of the Borders, a small town nestling under the triple peaks of the Eildon Hills, and the town that invented Rugby Sevens. The ruined abbey here is one of a handful across the Borders, a place often ravaged by invading English armies and the last resting place of the heart of King Robert the First. It is a place of serene beauty and malignant memories, yet in the 10 years that we lived in the Borders, in nearby Peebles, I did not hear about the vampire story. Perhaps the locals did not wish it to ruin the image of this outwardly peaceful little town.

The vampire story is straightforward. One of the monks at the abbey had not lived a blameless life, and heaven refused him. Although his colleagues buried him in the graveyard beside the abbey, he did not settle there but rose from the dead at night. Rather than tormenting the local farmers, this bloodsucking monk specialised in the women at a nearby nunnery. Why do vampires seem to prefer women? Is their blood sweeter than that of men? Or is there some sexual overtone?

The short version of the legend relates that the other monks became aware of this night-roaming pest, and one brave man patrolled the abbey grounds, armed with a huge axe. He waited until he saw the vampire rising from his grave then chopped off his head. No garlic, no stake through the heart, just a simple blow with an axe – that was the way in the old Border.

Naturally, some people do not believe that the issue ended there. According to the story, the vampire remains in the grounds of the abbey. As I said above, I had not heard of the creature when I lived in the area, and I occasionally worked in Melrose, with local men, none of whom mentioned knowing of a vampire monk. So who began this obscure little legend?

Well, it's an old story and, as far as I have been able to discover, has a single root. A 12th-century English historian named William of Newburgh wrote a volume called *Historia rerum Anglicarum*, which translates as *History of English Affairs*, which claims to be a history of England from 1066 to

1198. The subject matter wavers a bit and strays across the frontier into Scotland to talk of the Melrose vampire. William also mentions other similar stories from England, so perhaps such legends were accepted as history in the 12th century. In William's account, he says that the vampire monk was less than spiritual when alive, and the events occurred "a few years ago". Known as Hudreprest or Dog Priest because he liked dogs, the vampire monk also had a lover in Melrose and, after he was dead and buried, he roamed from his grave. The other monks were not alarmed by his appearances, so he called on his lover. However, she preferred a live monk to a dead one and ran to the abbey for help. Always willing to help a damsel in distress, four monks volunteered to guard the grave.

After a fruitless night, three of the monks retired back to the abbey, leaving a brave man on his own beside the grave. Luckily this lone man carried an axe, and dealt with the vampire, if it was a vampire, as he left the grave. The dead monk quickly retired below the ground, from where the monks dug him up. They discovered that the dead monk was in his grave, bleeding from the wound made by the axe. Lifting the body, the monks carried it out of the sanctified ground around the abbey and burned it, allowing the wind to take the ashes wherever it would.

Another version, probably from the same 12th-century source but twisted in the re-telling, also mentions the name Hunderprest. This version is the only one that claims the undead monk left his grave, turned into a bat and fluttered around the abbey walls, looking for an entrance. Rather than hacking at him with an axe, the monks resorted to the more peaceful, and probably more effective, method of praying for divine help. The prayers repelled the vampire, who flew into Melrose to find a woman who, in this version, had worked for him, although in what capacity it is hard to say. Nevertheless, the woman did not appreciate this vampire monk screaming outside her house and ran to Melrose Abbey for help. One of the monks had experience in this sort of thing – so it presumably had happened before – and dashed across to exorcise the unhappy spirit.

Here the stories merge for a while as the exorcist brought three other monks to help him in an overnight vigil. When night fell, the vampire monk rose from the grave, tossing aside the gravestone as if it were made of parchment. Possibly recognising the exorcist as the major threat, the vampire floated toward him. Used to such events, the exorcist fought back with his blessed staff, thumping the vampire until it retreated into its grave.

Aware that the vampire was hurt but not destroyed, the exorcist and his companions waited beside the grave until dawn, and then had the grave opened as silver sunlight slipped over the horizon. As in the previous stories, they lifted the bloodied corpse, removed it outside the abbey's sacred ground and burned it.

Some people are said to have heard the screams of the undead monk as he floats around the abbey grounds. Others have seen a group of long-departed monks patrolling around the gravestones, ensuring the vampire does not return.

Naturally, in a place 900 years old, there are various stories about Melrose Abbey. Michael Scott is said to be buried here. Scott was born about 1175, possibly in the Borders, perhaps in Fife. He was undoubtedly a scholar, an intellectual who studied at Oxford and Paris before travelling around Europe, translating books from Arabic into Latin. At that time a fragment of Outremer, the Crusader's conquests in the Holy Land existed, and Eastern knowledge fascinated Scott, so he dressed in Arab clothes and studied their knowledge and literature, which made him an object of suspicion in Christian Europe. He was a genuine intellectual, with his translations including an Arab work called *The Secret of Secrets* which may have been one cause for people thinking him a wizard.

Scott also studied astronomy, alchemy and the occult, so Frederick II, the Holy Roman Emperor and one of the most powerful of European monarchs, invited him to be become his court astrologer, a kind of Merlin and Arthur relationship. The Pope also used his skills. Scott crossed the Pyrenees into Spain, where the Christian kingdoms were still fighting to reconquer the country. In the vast library of Toledo, he translated the Arabic versions of Greek philosopher Aristotle's texts on natural sciences into Latin.

Scott is also said to have predicted that he would die by a stone falling on his head and so wore an iron helmet to protect himself. One day, while he was at Melrose, he removed his headgear for mass, and a stone fell on his head, killing him. In common with other supposed wizards, Scott was said to have a magic staff, using it to split the Eildon Hills in three, while he was also said to have learned how to fly and to have built Hadrian's Wall in a single day. It was Sir Walter Scott who reconstituted, or invented, the story that he is buried at a cross in the Melrose area, along with his books of magic. The cross, of course, would keep him safe from demonic powers, and also, presumably, from the Islamic knowledge that he brought to Europe. Michael Scott was either famous or infamous, depending on one's point of view, but he was sufficiently well known for Dante to include him in his *Inferno*, thrusting him into the eighth circle of Hell. In Scotland, of course, he is better remembered as the Borders Wizard and is said to haunt the ruins of Melrose Abbey.

Lastly, the abbey is also home to an unknown black thing, more like a shadow than anything tangible, which people have apparently seen slithering between the gravestones. Perhaps merely a shadow in the moonlight, but in a building with such a reputation, who knows?

THE WIZARD OF MERCHISTON

THE NAPIERS WERE A FORMIDABLE BREED. As well as the Napiers of Merchiston, there were the Napiers of Wrychtishouses, where Brunstfield is now. It was a William Napier, probably of Wrychtishouses, who held Edinburgh Castle against Henry IV when the English king invaded in the early years of the 15th century but now few people remember his name.

Wrychtishouses was one of the oldest and most picturesque buildings in Edinburgh, and at the end of the 18th century, Lieutenant-general Robertson of Lude lived here. Robertson was a soldier during the American War of Independence and, when it ended, he returned to Edinburgh with a man named Black Tom. Now Tom lived in a room on the ground floor of Wrychtishouses and slept very badly. He claimed that a headless woman emerged from the hearth, holding a baby. Naturally, nobody believed the word of a mere servant. Rather than investigate his story, General Robertson and others thought that Tom had been drinking and dismissed his tales.

Many years later, when improvers demolished the old

Wrychtishouses to erect what is now Gillespie's School, the builders tore away the hearthstone of Tom's old room. Underneath they found the skeleton of a fully dressed headless woman and a bundle wrapped in a pillowcase by her side. The builders opened the pillowcase with trembling fingers and found the body of a child. There was no known history attached to the pair, so their life and death will probably remain for ever a mystery.

Despite the abortive siege of Edinburgh Castle and the headless ghost, the name Napier was more famously associated with Merchiston in Edinburgh. Probably the most celebrated was John Napier, born in 1550 when his father was just 16 years old. Educated at St Andrews University, John Napier travelled to Europe to continue his studies. He was interested in the science and application of mathematics, a subject many people regarded with suspicion and, when he returned to Scotland, there were those who thought Napier was a necromancer. He also became involved in the war between the followers of King James VI and Queen Mary, with Mary's garrison in Edinburgh Castle bombarding Merchiston. Not surprisingly, with cannonballs wheeching past his head, Napier left Merchiston Castle until the fighting was over. When he returned, he resumed his studies, turning the battlements into an observatory as he added astrology to his interests, which furthered his reputation as a necromancer.

The citizens of Edinburgh began to believe all sorts of exciting things about Napier. They thought he had a black cockerel as a familiar and they believed he had supernatural powers and was in league with the Devil. Napier allowed these stories to spread and multiply. He possibly encouraged the superstitious beliefs so his less intellectual neighbours would leave him in peace. The stories claim that Napier told his neighbours that his black cockerel could find out all their secrets, which could be a terrible thing in a small community, and perhaps dangerous for Napier at a time that witch hunts were on the rise.

One story of John Napier claims that when a ring of his disappeared, he suspected one of his servants of having stolen it. He ordered all his servants to gather in the great hall of Merchiston Tower and said he would take them, one by one, into the darkest room, where he did his studying, and they had to stroke the back of his cockerel, which would crow when the guilty servant touched it.

The servants duly lined up and entered the room, and each time they did so, the bird remained silent until Napier had processed all the servants. Only then did Napier demand to see their hands. Only one of the servants had clean hands. The others were soiled by the soot with which Napier had smeared his bird. The guilty had condemned himself.

Edinburgh people called Napier the Warlock of the Tower, with his tricks and subterfuge as well as his mathematical skills and star-gazing. On another occasion, a flock of pigeons had been feasting on his crops, and he said he would poind them, which means capture them and sell them to make up for the damage.

Naturally, Napier's neighbours laughed at the idea. "Do so, if you can catch them," one mocked.

Napier put his mind to work, soaked a bucketload of peas in intoxicating spirits and spread them across his land. Next morning, he scooped up a hundred drunken pigeons. People called the area Doo Park (dove park) from that incident, according to the legend.

Napier's reputation spread far from Edinburgh so that, in the summer of 1594 he made a contract with Sir Robert Logan of Restalrig to try to find treasure supposedly hidden in Fast Castle, down on the Berwickshire coast. There is no record that anybody ever found the treasure, although Napier's reward was to be a third of the proceeds. Logan was also involved in the infamous Gowrie conspiracy of 1600, which proposed kidnapping King James VI at Gowrie House, taking him to Fast Castle and holding him prisoner there until orders came from Elizabeth of England, or somebody else, what to do with him.

Nobody found out about Logan's involvement in the Gowrie conspiracy until years after he died. When the authorities finally discovered the treason, they ordered gravediggers to dig up Logan's bones, which were taken into court for sentence. The court decreed that "the memorie and dignitie of the said Robert Logan be extinct and abolished" and his arms deleted from all books. His bones were reburied in Leith.

So who was this John Napier? He was the man who, in 1614, invented logarithms, that bane of every school pupil who does not have a natural bent for mathematics. So rather than being a wizard, he was a mathematical genius.

And with that mathematical wizard, we say farewell to that section of the book and move on to the next, strange old Edinburgh, my home town and a city like no other.

PART SIX
STRANGE EDINBURGH

DRINKING AND HAUNTING IN EDINBURGH'S PUBS

IN ALL MY TRAVELS, I have never been to a city that has such a variety of weird, quirky and downright strange public houses as Edinburgh. It is unarguable that the capital of Scotland has a plethora of public houses, or "publics" as people used to call them, a term that time shortened to the better known "pub." Some famous pub names have now gone, others remain, and even locals would often find it difficult to tell the story behind many.

The Boundary Bar in Leith Walk is now known as the Bier Hoose and serves German and Belgian beers. As the former name suggests, this pub sits squarely astride the boundary between Edinburgh and Leith, once two independent towns where the licensing hours once differed. The landlord in a now-gone era had a broad line painted through his pub, marking the border, and when the bell rang for time in the Edinburgh half, the patrons stepped en masse into the town of Leith for another half hour's imbibing.

Little touches like that make up the character of Edinburgh, which is fast disappearing, unfortunately.

In my opinion, and I admit I am biased having misspent my youth in such places, the Old Town, or Auld Toun, of Edinburgh, has some of the strangest pubs in Scotland. One of those is the World's End, if only for its name. In the Middle Ages, and especially in the troubled years following the Battle of Flodden in 1513, Edinburgh was a walled city. The city was much smaller then, extending halfway down the Royal Mile. Beyond the city walls, the separate Burgh of the Canongate reached as far as Holyrood Palace. At the city boundary was the Netherbow Port, which was a turreted gate, locked at night. Nestled beside the Netherbow, the last pub in Edinburgh gained its name of the World's End. To the people of Edinburgh, the world ended at the city boundary.

Stockbridge, old Stockaree where I grew up, once possessed what was undoubtedly my favourite pub name, if not my favourite pub. The Silver Buckle commemorated Walter Ross, a kindly landlord who claimed to have set man-traps for poachers but was in reality too soft-hearted to harm anybody. When his lands were constantly poached, Ross visited the infirmary and obtained an amputated leg. He paraded it around his grounds, asking for the owner, so he could return the silver buckle on the shoe and displaying his ruthlessness at the same time. I don't know if the poaching stopped, but the incident typifies the local slant on history that pub names should recall.

Ross was an interesting man who lived in the latter decades of the 18th century. On the land where Anne Street now stands, he built a 40-foot-high tower which became known as Ross's Folly and incorporated masonry from Edinburgh's many ruined old buildings in the walls. Ross climbed up the folly by an outside stair and used the upper storey as a summer house. The folly was destroyed in 1825 when Anne Street was extended.

The Last Drop in the Grassmarket is in the shadow of

the castle and only yards from where Burke and Hare preyed on the unfortunates, destitute and gullible to sell the bodies to Knox the anatomist. The name shows Edinburgh's macabre humour, for the establishment is directly opposite one of the capital's places of execution. In the centre of the Grassmarket, scores, perhaps hundreds, of people took their final step to the last drop and choked to death on the end of a rope.

Nevertheless, it is not one of the unfortunate victims who haunts the pub, but a little girl who lived in the flat above, or perhaps in the building before it became a pub. She is said to wear mediaeval clothing, so must be a few hundred years old despite her youthful appearance.

Another Edinburgh pub connected to hanging is Deacon Brodie's Tavern in the High Street. Brodie lived in the 18th century, being born in 1741, and was outwardly a picture of respectability. Deacon of the Guild of Wrights and a town councillor, he was one of the most skilled carpenters in Edinburgh and mingled with the elite of the city, meeting many famous men including Robert Burns the poet and Henry Raeburn the artist. Yet Brodie was an oxymoron, like Edinburgh itself. He used his day job to size up houses to rob, made copies of locks and doors and at night went on the prowl. When he was not gambling or seducing one or other of his mistresses, he was thieving until he was finally caught and hanged in 1788.

He grew up in Brodie's Close in the Lawnmarket, and he was a wright and undertaker along with his brothers. It is also said that Brodie designed a new type of gallows for Edinburgh. Brodie began his criminal career with a bank job in 1768 and by 1786 headed a small but professional gang. The shopkeepers used to hang their keys on a nail on the back of their doors. Brodie carried a piece of putty in the palm of his hand

and make impressions of the keys, then employed a blacksmith to make copies of keys.

Brodie's last attempt was on the Excise Office in Chessel's Court in the Canongate, and when that proved abortive one of his gang, a man named Brown, turned King's Evidence and gave away two more of Brodie's accomplices. Brodie fled to the Netherlands, was captured and returned to Edinburgh for trial. Found guilty, Brodie and one of his accomplices, Smith, were hanged at the Tolbooth in October 1788, with 40,000 spectators watching – and that is when the strange rumours began.

There were stories that Brodie had survived the hanging. People said that he had manufactured a steel collar, so the rope had not choked him. Rumours abounded that he had bribed the hangman not to notice the collar, and his friends carried away his body and revived him. People said that his grave in St Cuthbert's Chapel of Ease was empty. Others denied the rumours, saying he had been adequately hanged and was dead and gone. Yet if so, how was he later seen in Paris?

The legend lived on and intrigued Robert Louis Stevenson so his famous character, Dr Jekyll (with his alter ego Hyde), was reputed to be based on the deacon.

Another worthwhile pub is the Tolbooth Tavern, down the Canongate toward Holyrood. The situation could not be more historic as the Canongate Tolbooth is itself a fascinating building. Built in 1591, when the Canongate was a separate burgh, the tollbooth was the building where tolls were collected, as well as being the court, burgh chambers and prison.

The man who had the Canongate Tolbooth built, Sir Lewis Bellenden, was also the Justice Clerk who, according to legend, once interrogated a wizard who later died in custody. In 1820, the lower front part of the building became a pub, today the Tolbooth Tavern, but some of the old memories remain. According to the stories, some spirit haunts the pub, toppling bottles and glasses, while the staff glimpse something, or someone, at an open door upstairs. The spirit may be of one of the men held prisoner when the Tolbooth was a prison, while a pair of long-dead old soldiers also visit.

The Star. This small place in Northumberland Place is diagonally opposite where I used to live. Although my wife and I were regulars there back in the early 1980s, I had no idea of the strange stories attached to it. This pub boasts a human skull on the premises, with a clause in the lease saying the skull must remain in the building. Apparently, if anybody removed the skull, they or the pub suffered a disaster – fire or flood, not to mention a shooting, which is incredibly unusual in Edinburgh.

The White Hart Inn is another historic public house in the Grassmarket, with a cellar that is said to date back to 1516. Strange things have happened in the White Hart, from figures appearing in photographs to invisible fingers touching members of staff, while some drinkers have also heard footsteps. Burke and Hare, the mass murderers, may have operated from this site in the 1820s. That alone is undoubtedly sufficient to give any pub notoriety.

The Banshee Labyrinth, in Niddry Street, is said to be Scotland's most haunted pub. One story, which has several versions, says that when a group of tradesmen were renovating the place they heard a woman sobbing. After a search, they found a young woman cradling her head in her hands. When the tradesmen asked if she was all right, the woman raised her head, to reveal a face with no eyes, and she screamed so loudly that the men beat a hasty retreat right out of the pub and into the street. There is another story that a gentleman named Lord Nicol Edwards, one-time Lord Provost of Edinburgh, lived where part of the pub now stands. According to legend, Edwards not only abused his wife but also tortured witches in this building. Now Edwards may have existed, but he was not the Lord Provost, according to the list I consulted. Anybody who knows more about these stories is welcome to comment!

Maggie Dickson's is a pub in the Grassmarket, which tells a strange and perhaps true tale. Margaret Dickson was a fish hawker in the early years of the 18th century, one of many in old Edinburgh. She came from Inveresk, by Musselburgh, but in 1722 or 1723 when she was about 20 years old, her husband left her to work in the keels at Newcastle. Another version of the story has the Royal Navy pressganging her man. Moving away from the city, Margaret settled in Kelso in the Scottish Borders, where she found a job with an innkeeper. She also found that she liked the innkeeper's son and, nature taking its course, Maggie became pregnant.

With unmarried pregnancy a shameful thing in the 18th century, Margaret tried to conceal her state as long as possible. The child came prematurely and, like so many babies in these precarious times, he died within a few days. Margaret at first intended throwing her dead baby into the River Tweed but instead, left the tiny body on the bank of the river. Naturally, somebody found the baby, and fingers soon pointed to Margaret.

Taken to Edinburgh and tried under the 1690 Concealment of Pregnancy Act, Margaret was convicted and sentenced to death by hanging. The execution took place in the Grassmarket on 2 September 1724, with John Dalgliesh, the hangman making a slight mistake in not tying her hands. However, although Margaret tried to loosen the noose, Dalgliesh quickly pinioned her arms, allowing her to hang for the allotted time and hauling at her legs to hasten the end. When the crowd began to drift away, Margaret was cut down and placed in a coffin, which, as was the custom, was placed ready at the foot of the gibbet.

There were a few frantic moments when a group of

surgeon-apprentices tried to grab Margaret's body for dissection, and her friends repelled them with fist and boot. With that scare survived, the unhappy group placed the coffin in a cart, which jolted away on the road to Musselburgh. Perhaps it was the motion of the cart, but something stirred in Margaret and she woke to find herself inside a closed coffin, which must have been more than a little scary. When Margaret began to kick and struggle, the noise she made alerted her friends, and when they reached Peffermill for much-needed refreshment, they wrenched open the lid to find her alive. By the time the cart reached Musselburgh, possibly with Margaret walking much of the journey, the executed woman was back to full fitness.

There remained the matter of the law, of course. However, in this instance, the authorities tempered justice with mercy. According to the lawyers, the executioner had hanged Maggie, and that was the end of the matter. God had saved her, so she lived another 40 years with the name "half-hangit Maggie Dickson" as a salt seller and alehouse keeper. Maggie had a few more children, with her legal husband, while stories circulated that she used her evident good looks to charm the rope-maker into supplying a weak rope to the executioner.

That was only a small sample from a long list. Indeed, it would be difficult to find a pub in old Edinburgh that did not have a story or was not named after a happening. From Ensign Ewart's, beside the castle, that commemorates an incident at the 1815 Battle of Waterloo to the Persevere in Leith that boasts the motto of old, independent Leith, stories abound. However, Edinburgh is not only about pubs. There are many more strange things in the city.

EDINBURGH SECRETS

As I have suggested, there is nowhere quite like Edinburgh, Scotland's oxymoronic capital city. The strange old heart, between the Castle and the Palace of Holyroodhouse, has roots that extend at least to the Middle Ages. Although altered by time and man, the Auld Toun retains much of the mediaeval layout, with a single central street with numerous closes and wynds running down the ridge on either side. To the north and south of this Auld Toun – or Old Town if you are not an Edinburgher – is the New Town of elegant squares, terraces and private pleasure gardens. These two, combined, made up the Edinburgh of Robert Louis Stevenson that tormented genius of a writer, who drew the duality of his home city into many of the novels his cunning hand created.

There is a story in every five steps in the New Town and every step in the Auld. Even the walls of the Auld Toun have a story to tell, for spikes topped the gates, and on these spikes – known as pricks – the authorities impaled the heads of decapitated criminals, traitors and those whom the authorities disliked or of whom they disapproved.

One of the strangest things about Edinburgh is the fact that it still exists, being fewer than 60 miles from the border with one of the most predatory nations in Europe, if not the world. As an example of the danger in which Edinburgh constantly survived, here is an abridged order of King Henry VIII of England to the Earl of Hertford in 1544, during the wars of the Rough Wooing:

Put all to fire and sword, burn Edinburgh town, so razed and defaced when you have sacked and gotten what ye can of it as there may remain forever a perpetual memory of the vengeance of God for their falsehood and disloyalty... beat down and overthrow the Castle, sack Holyrood House and as many towns and villages as ye conveniently can; sack Leith, burn and subvert it, putting man woman and child to the sword, without exception, when any resistance shall be made against you.

The Scots resisted, of course, with the burghers of Edinburgh raising their Blue Blanket standard in defiance and repulsing the initial English assault at Leith Wynd Port. When the invaders battered their way in with artillery, and fire and blood despoiled the streets of the capital, individuals sold their lives dearly. One such was David Halkerston who took his two-handed sword and fought the invaders outside the lane that became Halkerston's Wynd. Although the city fell, Hertford's assault on the castle failed, with hundreds of the attackers killed, and the English retreated to take out their frustration on the undefended villages of Midlothian.

Central to life in Edinburgh, as in every Scottish burgh, was the Mercat Cross. Here the Lord Provost made proclamations that affected everybody, and merchants made their deals.

In 1513, Edinburgh's Mercat Cross was the scene of one of the strangest events even in its long history. At that time, King James IV was on the throne, and Scotland was enjoying a period of prosperity and peace. King James was one of the most talented and energetic kings Scotland ever had, a renaissance monarch of the highest order. Unfortunately, James was also a hopeless romantic, as oxymoronic a king as Edinburgh is a city. Although James's wife was English, he was also king of a nation allied to France, the Auld Alliance that had been in place since 1295. When England attacked France, the French appealed for Scottish help, and King James hastened to be loyal to his commitment. One story says that Queen Anne of France sent James a ring, appealing to his famed chivalry.

Not everybody in Scotland wished to break the peace with England, but loyalty demanded a response, so the Scottish army gathered. According to one legend related by Robert Lindsay of Pitscottie, at midnight before the army set off and warriors packed Edinburgh, unseen trumpets sounded a fanfare and a red glow spread across the street. Amid the glare, a horned demon named Plotcock appeared at the Mercat Cross. When Plotcock read out a list of the men who would die in the forthcoming battle of Flodden, a former Lord Provost of Edinburgh, Richard Lawson, heard his name called. Pulling out a silver groat, marked with a cross, Lawson threw it at the demon in an appeal to live. Plotcock vanished and, according to the legend, Lawson fought at Flodden and survived the slaughter.

There was a Richard Lawson of High Riggs, Cairnmuir, Cambo and Boghall. He was Lord Justice Clerk from 1488 to 1491 and Provost of Edinburgh in 1492, but he may have died in 1507, six years before the battle of Flodden.

There is a similar story about a warning in Linlithgow, where Pitscottie tells of the king sitting in St Michael's Kirk, "verie sad and dollarous", (very sad and dolorous) when a strange apparition appeared before him. A man dressed in blue warned James not to invade England and then it "vanishit away... as he had bene ane blink of the sone or ane quhipe of the whirle wind". (Vanished away as he had been a blink of the sun or whip of the whirlwind.) Possibly these incidents were supernatural, yet there is also a theory that some members of the nobility were attempting to warn King James against waging war. The first campaign of that conflict ended in disaster at the battle of Flodden.

There have been hundreds of battles and skirmishes fought between Scotland and England, or between the people who lived in these nations before they assumed their current names. The vast majority have been forgotten, so it is unlikely that many people could name more than a dozen.

One that people remember is Flodden, fought in 1513. The result was a national catastrophe that crippled Scotland, with many of her nobles and thousands of her men killed. The battle was so horrendous that myths and legends grew from the bloody grass, one being that King James IV did not die with his men and was waiting to return and lead Scotland again. There are tales that a Scottish merchant in Tournai had spoken to the king, while Lindsay of Pitscottie wrote of a myth that four horsemen rescued James, placed him on a "dun hackney" and rode away. Another legend claimed that James had survived the carnage and sailed away on a pilgrimage, presumably to the Holy Land. Sadly the truth was less romantic. King James the IV, that most talented of monarchs, died in the battle.

According to legend, James had repeatedly been warned not to lead his army to war, even to help an old ally against the auld enemy. Augmenting the demon in Edinburgh and the man in blue who warned him at Linlithgow, there was a hare that ran from his tent and which his knights could not catch. Hares were well-known to be witches and therefore, a portent of disaster. When mice chewed at the leather fastenings of James' helmet and red dew covered his tent, James knew fate was against him. Yet even with the animals and spirits of nature giving due warning, James still marched to defeat.

Edinburgh is home to many secrets, some of which people have long forgotten. For example, there is said to be a secret path up the Castle Rock, which only the garrison knew. During the First War of Independence, when an English garrison occupied the castle, a Scotsman named William Frank volunteered to lead a Scottish force up the rock to retake the castle.

At first sight, the rock is impossible except for trained mountaineers or perhaps Royal Marine Commandos. However, while he was a member of the garrison, Frank had climbed down the Rock to meet his girl. He knew the secret route.

On the stormy night of 14 March 1312, Frank guided a picked team of 30 soldiers up the rock. As far as can be ascertained, his route began on the north side, above the present Princes Street Castle, underneath a feature known as Wallace's Cradle, or the Crane Bastion. Commanded by Randolph, Earl of Moray, the Scots scaled the rock, slid over the castle wall and defeated the English defenders.

After that assault, the path returned to obscurity until 1821 when, some 70 feet above Wallace's Cradle, workmen found faint steps carved in the rock. Perhaps a rope, or rope ladder, was suspended to the ground from the end of the steps.

Edinburgh Castle has many other secrets, including the ghostly drummer who appeared before the civil wars of the mid-17th century. Like all the best stories, it started on a cloudy night, when a lone sentry stood on the ramparts and heard the ominous tapping of a drum on the esplanade. When he leaned over the battlements to see what was happening, he saw nobody at first but heard the marching of many feet. Thinking the castle was under threat, the sentry fired his musket, which was a prearranged signal of alarm. When the garrison commander, Colonel Dundas, hurried out to see what the trouble was and saw no attacking army, he had the sentry beaten and replaced.

No sooner had the next sentinel started his rounds than he also heard the tapping of a drum and the rhythmic marching of hundreds of feet. Following orders, he fired his musket, which brought Colonel Dundas, bleary-eyed and grumpy, to the battlements for a second time. Again the colonel heard nothing.

Sending the second sentry away, Dundas took the man's musket, loaded it, hunched his shoulders against the ever-present wind and began to walk the prescribed beat. Alone on the battlements, he heard the old Scots march, the rhythm that the veterans of the Thirty Years War had used to unnerve their enemies. Like his predecessors on that station, Dundas leaned over the battlements to see the drummer. There was nobody there, although Dundas heard the distinct crunch of marching feet and the rattle of equipment, as though an invisible army was marching into the castle. As Dundas listened, the drums altered to the English march, then the French and finally, one he did not recognise at all but which was later used by Oliver Cromwell.

Nobody ever knew who the phantom army was, although it seems to have been a warning of the horrors to come when the Civil War engulfed all four nations within the British Isles.

Another secret is held in plain sight, visited by hundreds of people each day the castle is open. The Scottish Crown Jewels, more officially the Honours of Scotland, are the oldest in Britain and include a mace and sceptre, both surmounted by a sizeable crystal beryl. According to legend, the beryl was the badge of the archdruid, and maybe the clach-bhuai, or stone of power. If so, then the beryl might be 1,000 years old or more. On the other hand, it may be only a few hundred. One legend claims that by owning the clach-bhuai, the Scottish monarchs were protected from the powers of the druids.

When Cromwell ransacked and butchered his way across Scotland, loyal Scots hid the Honours from him, taking them initially to Dunnottar Castle on the northeast coast. Cromwell's armies followed, and the 70-strong Scottish garrison held out for eight months. When it became apparent Cromwell's army would capture the castle, willing hands lowered the Honours over the walls to the beach below, where a serving woman carried then to Kinneff Church, a few miles away. The minister, James Grainger, and his wife first hid them in their bed, then buried them in the church, periodically checking them. Cromwell's occupying army could not find them.

In 1660, King Charles II returned to the throne and the Honours came back to Edinburgh Castle. They came out for air to represent the next series of kings, who did not bother to visit Scotland but remained in England, and in 1707, with the Union of the Parliaments, the Honours were hidden away in a box in a locked room. And there they remained until Walter Scott, the Wizard of the North, traced them and had them unearthed in 1818. One likes to think that the old-time druid smiled as his crystal orb saw daylight again.

There are many other half-hidden secrets, of course. For instance, in Gosford's Close off the Lawnmarket, the Abbot of Cambuskenneth once owned his townhouse. The lowest storey had an arched cellar, which itself held a trap door, cunningly hidden, leading to a dungeon-style chamber hacked from the rock. There were once many stories about this dungeon, which was reputed to be a torture chamber. However, it was more likely to have been a storage area for goods smuggled across the Nor Loch, the moat that defended Edinburgh to the north, where Princes Street Gardens now spreads. More prosaic perhaps, but still a bit strange for an abbot.

There was another hidden room on the Castle Hill, where stood a crazy collection of buildings that once had been the home of Mary of Guise, widow of King James V. When the building was destroyed in 1846, men discovered a previously unknown chamber on the first floor. With a narrow window into Nairne's Close the only source of light, the room had an inventive sliding panel to a narrow turnpike staircase. The room was so secret that there are no stories or legends associated with it.

Another nearly-forgotten secret concerns Craigmillar Castle, on the southern outskirts of the city. In 1813 two gentlemen, John Pinkerton, an advocate, and Mr Irvine, a Writer to the Signet, were exploring the dungeons and found a human skeleton bricked up in a standing position inside the wall. There seems to be no clue as to the identity of the unfortunate victim, but there is a story that, before the discovery, visitors to the castle smelled lavender in the great hall, which apparently proved the presence of ghosts.

The only suspected-and-named ghost in Craigmillar Castle is Mary, Queen of Scots, who drifts around in the dress of a Green Lady, while other vague tales mention a long tunnel between the castle and Peffermill House. Queen Mary was often in the area, which gives a little plausibility to the claim her ghost remained. Edinburgh remains a city of secrets, so no doubt more will creep to the surface as the centuries slide past.

MARY KING'S CLOSE

A DIFFERENT AND less royal Mary is involved in probably the most famous haunted site in Edinburgh. Mary King's Close is the subject of a hundred stories, rumours, fables, myths and downright lies. The close, or rather the labyrinth of underground passages, rooms and chambers, have been the subject of curiosity and superstitious fear for generations.

Mary King appears to have been the widow of a merchant in the early part of the 17th century. Around 1645, when civil war had ravaged Scotland for years, a plague hit Edinburgh and killed hundreds, perhaps thousands of people. Mary King's Close suffered along with the rest and, according to some accounts, was closed off or partially deserted. Possibly this isolation helped fund the stories that claimed people had seen headless bodies dancing around the close, and said a minister and two kirk elders had fled from a floating head and severed arm dripping with blood that emerged from a solid wall.

As far back as the 18th century, when the close was open to the skies, boys would dare each other to visit. They shouted through the keyholes and ran away in case the plague, which the boys believed was confined in the old closed-off houses, escaped into the teeming tenements of the capital. In 1685 a book named *Satan's Invisible Work Discovered* mentioned that a solicitor named Thomas Coltheart leased or bought a house in the close, but his maid refused to work in such a haunted place.

Mr and Mrs Coltheart were in their bedroom one Sunday afternoon when Mrs Coltheart looked up from her Bible to see the disembodied head of an old man floating in the air, watching her. Not unnaturally, Mrs Coltheart fainted, and her husband told her she had imagined the vision. They went to bed that night, and a few moments later Coltheart saw the same floating head, staring at him.

Probably frightened and undoubtedly brave, Coltheart lit a candle and began to pray, only for a child to join the head, and shortly afterwards, an arm. Determined to face down these strange apparitions, Coltheart asked them to tell him their story so he could help them rest, without effect. Instead, other spiritual creatures joined the array, including a dog, which lay on a chair, a cat and more and more apparitions of unnatural form until they filled the room. Once the whole crowd was there, Coltheart heard a deep groan, and then the unwelcome guests vanished.

According to the story, the Colthearts did not flee the house but remained there until Mr Coltheart's death, without seeing any more apparitions. However, on the day of his death, his image appeared to a friend in Tranent.

"Are you dead?" asked the friend, "and if so, what is your errand?"

When the image of Coltheart shook his head and vanished, the gentleman rode to Mary King's Close to find Mrs Coltheart in tears and her man dead.

Again the house lay deserted for a while until a married ex-soldier took it over. At midnight on the first night of their stay, their candle burned with a blue flame, and the floating head again appeared, sending the new tenants out of the close.

In 1753 part of the Close was demolished when the Royal Exchange was built. A century later, Cockburn Street rose on the ruins of the northern portion of the Close. Today what remains is a spooky visitor attraction that hundreds of visitors and locals visit as actors recreate life in the long-abandoned Close.

EDINBURGH WITCHES

I WAS TEMPTED to put this little piece in the witchcraft section but decided that it added more to Edinburgh's character instead. Restalrig Loch featured in the 1576 witch trial of a woman named Bessie Dunlop. According to Bessie, she was beside the loch when: "There came ane company of riders by, that made sic a din as if heaven and earth had gane together." Bessie's contact, a man named Tam Reid, told her the riders were "the Gude Wights, that were riding in middle-eard" (gude people, ie fairies or witches, who were riding in middle earth). As Tam Reid died at the Battle of Pinkie in 1547, Bessie's information seems dubious, at best but in these days of the late 16th century, Bessie's confession was enough to condemn her to death.

Another area known for witchcraft was the Loan of Broughton, a narrow lane between high hedges that led down the slope from the northern side of Calton Hill to the village of Broughton. What remains is known as Broughton Street.

In the late 16th century the feudal superior of Broughton was Sir Lewis Bellenden, who was known for his dealings with witches and warlocks. He died in November 1606 and his son Sir William Bellenden took over as Baron of Broughton. Unlike his father, Sir William incarcerated the local witches in the old tollbooth, with its 13 steps and stocks, which stood at the east end of present Barony Street.

If the legends are true, Sir William was not a merciful man, for in December 1608 he questioned and tried a coven of Broughton witches. Although they denied the charges, Sir William found them guilty and burned them alive, which was highly unusual in Scotland. It would be a horrible sight as some broke free of the flames and the executioners, or perhaps the crowd, threw them back into the fire. Today Broughton Street is a busy thoroughfare of small shops and packed pubs, with no memory of those troubled times.

THE FATAL TOUCH

In old Scotland, there was a long-held belief that if a man murdered somebody, his touch on the corpse would cause the wound to bleed again. This superstition has no scientific evidence, but it seems that on at least one occasion that belief condemned a man to the gallows.

Some time in the latter half of the 17th century, an Englishman named Sir James Stanfield moved to Newmills in East Lothian. In common with the best sort of Englishmen, he was hard-working, God-fearing and a good neighbour, so the people of East Lothian accepted him, and he became well liked. His son was the opposite, a wilful, arrogant and ignorant man who caused trouble wherever he went. And then, in November 1687, a local farmer found Sir James Stanfield's body in a pond near his house.

Suicide was the immediate conclusion – a terrible act brought on by a melancholic state of mind. But soon doubts crept in and people began to talk, as country folk do.

However decent a man Sir James seemed to be, there were dark tales of domestic troubles and people wondered how his wife, Lady Stanfield, knew to have his grave-clothes prepared before he died. Also, suspicious neighbours asked, why was he buried so quickly after his death? What was the family hiding?

A couple of learned surgeons rode out from Edinburgh to Newmills to investigate the matter. Digging up the body after it had been two days underground, the surgeons took it to a church and examined it thoroughly. They soon decided that Sir James had been strangled, rather than drowned. Washing the body, the surgeons wrapped it gently in clean linen before putting it in a coffin. Two men lifted the body, James Row, an Edinburgh merchant, and Philip Stanfield, Sir James's son.

Philip seemed to be the very opposite of his father. He was a womanising spendthrift who angered the good people of East Lothian and acted so foully that Sir James disinherited him. Indeed, it was rumoured that his son's actions that drove Sir James to depression and talks of suicide. Philip was present when surgeons examined his father's body, and the second that Philip put his hands on Sir James, the corpse began to bleed profusely.

"Lord, have mercy on me!" Philip said, immediately recognising the seriousness of the event. Stepping back from his father, he ran into the church office, gasping and groaning in horror. A crowd gathered, watching as Philip refused to go near the body again.

To the locals, it appeared evident that Philip had murdered his father so, in February 1688, the authorities questioned Sir James's servants about the seepage of blood. While under torture, the servants claimed that Philip had drunk to the confusion of King James VII, combined the king's name with the Devil, the pope and the Lord Chancellor while cursing Sir James. After that, Philip stood before a judge and jury, but the verdict was a foregone conclusion.

Philip said he was innocent, pointing out that his father

suffered from fits of melancholia and had already tried to commit suicide on at least one other occasion. However, it was no good, and the public executioner hanged Philip at the Mercat Cross. Not only that, but the hangman also cut out his tongue as the penalty for cursing his father and chopped off the hand that struck the fatal blow. After a painful, prolonged hanging, Philip died, the hangman chopped off his head and thrust it on a spike on the East Port of Haddington.

The only evidence against Philip was the blood on his hands when he handled the corpse of Sir James. Thank goodness today's rules of evidence are more reliable.

And with the end of Philip, we leave Strange Edinburgh and look at the stones that act as silent evidence to some of the strangest tales that Scotland can offer.

PART SEVEN
STRANGE TALES OF THE STONES

INTRODUCTION

As ANYBODY who has ever tried to dig a garden in Scotland will know, this is a country of stones and rock. The hills are of uncompromising granite; the towns are stone-built and as dour as the weather while even the people can be stony-faced on occasion. Yet some Scottish stones are as evocative as a whisper from a long-forgotten past as they rear up from purple-brown moorland under the sombre northern sky. Others protrude from damp fields without placard or explanation, are built into town walls or merely lie in strange places, lichen-furred with neglect as the old stories fade into obscurity and people race in an urgent dash to oblivion. Some talented person said that a nation with no past is fortunate. That may be true, yet a country that forgets its past is denying itself a soul. Scotland's soul is written in stone, tainted and stained perhaps, but all the more human for that. There are so many significant stones in Scotland that it is hard to make a selection, but in this small chapter, I have picked out some personal favourites. Scots being the disputatious people that they are, most people will disagree with my choice, arguing hotly that this stone or that circle is better. Good. Healthy debate can only enhance the subject and bring other stones into more general knowledge and perhaps help preserve those that matter.

THE SHINING ONE

I will start with arguably the most famous of all Scotland's stones, the great circle at Callanish (Calanais) on the west coast of the Island of Lewis in the Outer Hebrides. I had been working in Stornoway the first time I met the Stones of Callanish, and Cathy and I arrived on a grey, blustery day where the wind dragging ragged clouds across an angry sky intensified the atmosphere of the place. Many remnants of the distant past enhance this area, with more than one stone circle set among the heather moor and beside the little village of Callanish. Archaeologists have dated the main circle here to about 2600 BC, with an alignment that could allow worship of the moon or the stars, for celestial bodies fascinated the ancient inhabitants of Scotland. The main circle here is much more than a simple ring, more like a Celtic cross with a long stone corridor leading to the circle, that has arms pointing east, west and south. The off-central monolith is 4.8 metres high. It dwarfed my wife when I took a photograph of her standing in front of it.

Local people undoubtedly used Callanish for centuries, and the burial chamber at the heart of the stones antedates the original foundation by many years. Perhaps 1,000 years after they were erected, the Callanish stones were abandoned. The climate had cooled and layers of peat gradually formed over the area.

Unlike the stones in some other sites, the stones in Callanish were locally sourced, Lewisian gneiss, rough to the touch, lichen- and weather-stained. They belong in this environment, rearing up from the earth as if thrusting to a timeless god. However, when the Neolithic people erected the circle, Scotland's climate was less harsh, with milder winters, more trees in the area and the sea level lower. The local people were hunters and farmers, living what was probably a pretty comfortable existence for the time.

So much for history. As can be expected, many legends attach to Callanish, such as the old story that the stones were originally giants who roamed Lewis in the period before Christianity. When St Kieran arrived to spread the Gospel in Lewis, the giants refused Christianity, so Kieran turned them to stone, in a Christian-like manner of course.

Another tale, and one that I like, is the story of the Shining One. Midsummer has always been an important time for people who lived with nature, and one Callanish story claims that, when the sun rises on Midsummer Day, a cuckoo calls and a mysterious Shining One appears, walking along the avenue to the circle. This strange visitor may be a memory of some ancient rite, or merely an alternative name for the sun. It is equally possible it is the moon for, according to one Professor Alexander Thom, in midsummer the avenue is in line with the setting moon. Perhaps modern people view it backside-forward.

Cuckoos come into other Callanish legends with one such bird conveniently arriving to open the Beltane festivities. According to the story, when cuckoos fly from the mainland to Lewis in the spring, they first visit Callanish and give their distinctive call to announce their arrival, or to call the folk to worship at the Stones.

In her book *The Outer Hebrides and Their Legends*, Otta Swire relates another legend, that the stones are not indigenous to Lewis. In that story, a priest-king, accompanied by a gaggle of other priests and a company of "black men" arrived by ship, carrying the stones, which they set up in their present formation. While they were on Lewis, the priest-king was never seen without a flock of wrens, while the lesser priests wore cloaks made from coloured feathers.

After a short while, the priest-king sent most of the rest away and remained on Lewis with only a handful of the lesser priests. This priest-king started a new religion based on the stones. Was there any truth in this legend? Did a visitor to Lewis establish a new religion at some murky past time?

Folk memory is a fickle thing, with traditions that alter through time, and these stones are so old that the real meaning was lost centuries ago. Perhaps waves of invaders, Picts (unless they were descended from the original builders), Gaels and Norsemen, intermarried with the indigenous people and diluted the knowledge. Add Christian teaching, pagan Norse stories and centuries of intermittent warfare, and it is not surprising the stories are garbled.

According to one tradition, people included the stones in a fire festival that centred on the Celtic festival of Beltane, which occurred on the first day of May. On that day, every household in Lewis extinguished their fires, while one priest (druid or Christian?) started a new fire within the Callanish circle. Using this Callanish fire, he distributed flame to all the households of the island – which must have been tricky on a windy day. There may also have been a tradition for local people to visit the Stones on Celtic holy days, despite the disapproval of the Church. Nevertheless, it is a long leap between Celtic druids and the Neolithic builders of Callanish. Only folk traditions can do such things, particularly when history is hazy about both sets of people and can only surmise what they think is correct.

Over the centuries, a metre and a half of peat formed to conceal the actual size of the stones, although garbled remnants of the old stories must have remained. In 1857, the Victorians began a feverish campaign of archaeology to investigate the ancient past and revealed the true scale of Callanish. In this case, the Victorian in question was Sir James Matheson of the Jardine Matheson Company, a man who built Lews Castle in Stornoway, cleared hundreds of people from Lewis to Canada and was governor of the Bank of England as well as a large-scale opium dealer.

Only three years later, a local man, John Morrisone claimed the stones were men "converted into stone by ane enchanter".

Near to Callanish I, are two supporting circles, imaginatively named Callanish II and Callanish III, both of which are worth half an hour of anybody's time. The main site has a visitor centre with a shop and café.

Best time to visit? That depends on the visitor's reason for coming. The site can get busy with tourist buses in high season, so possibly come early to see the stones rearing up in the half-light of dawn when the surrounding moorland is barely visible. Or if you are fortunate, visit when a full moon is glossing the sky and a fitful Hebridean wind howls between the ancient monuments, stand in the centre of the circle and wonder if the Shining One may come.

I made mention of the moon with relation to Callanish, and the phases of the moon were essential for work in old rural Scotland. For example, farmers believed that the crescent moon encouraged growth, so planted crops or sowed seeds then, but not onions or kale, though, as they would run to seed.

When the moon was waning, men in the Hebrides tended

not to slaughter cattle, pigs, goats or sheep. They believed that flesh tasted bland at that time. It was also inadvisable to cut hazel or willow, which people used for baskets and creels. When the moon waned, men would not cut down trees for boat-building, for they believed that the sap withdrew into the roots, leaving the wood brittle. However, a waning moon was best for ploughing, cutting peat and harvesting, for the wisdom of the time claimed the moisture departed with the moon.

People would also start a journey on a crescent moon and Orkney marriages were best when the moon was waxing – when it was growing towards a full moon.

Moon worship was widespread in old Scotland, with the standing stones of Stennis in Orkney believed to have a circle of the sun and a semi-circle of the crescent moon.

The Picts seemed to continue this belief for one of their symbols, present across Scotland in later times, was two crescent moons back to back. Academics have interpreted this symbol as the last quarter of the waning moon and the first quarter of the waxing moon. It seems to be a sign of immortality – the rebirth after death. Perhaps that is why horned animals were held sacred and often sacrificed, as the curve of the horns mirrored the crescent of the moon. Such actions occurred as late as 1695 in Dingwall, less than 330 years ago – the past is only just under the surface.

THE CURSED STONES OF ROTHIEMURCHUS

AT THE BACK end of the 14th century, King Robert III was concerned about an ugly feud between two Highland clans, Clan Chattan and Clan Quhele. Clan Chattan is well-known, the Confederation of the Cat from Badenoch, including MacPherson, Mackintosh, and Shaw. Clan Quhele remains a mystery although, given later events, it may have been the Camerons, the "fiercer than fierce" warriors from Lochaber. Other people believe the second clans was the Davidsons of Inverhavon, who later joined Clan Chattan.

The king, being a practical sort of man, arranged a battle between 30 picked champions of each clan. The two companies met at the North Inch of Perth in September 1396, with Robert, his queen and royal court among the spectators. In this bloody gladiatorial contest, Clan Chattan emerged as the victors.

The captain of the Chattans in this epic encounter was a Shaw, known variously as Seath Mor or Farquhar Shaw. In 1405, this Shaw warrior died, and his people buried him in the graveyard at Rothiemurchus, then the traditional burial place of the Shaw family.

The grave is still visible in a special enclosure, marked with five stones known as the Homing Stones. One stone sits on each corner of the grave slab, and the fifth occupies the centre. These stones are significant, because they are cursed, or rather, they carry a curse that will fall on anybody who takes them away. They also wax and wane like the moon, with the fortunes of the Shaw family, according to the story.

One version of the story claims that a brownie, or perhaps a familiar spirit known as the Bodach an Duin – the Old Man of the Dun – looked after the Shaws when that family owned Rothiemurchus. In time, the powerful Grant family took over Rothiemurchus and the Shaws left, with the brownie following to look after the Shaw dead. Possibly it is the Bodach who puts the curse on anybody who removes the stones – and the wrath of a brownie is not to be scorned!

To give a couple of examples. In the same graveyard are the tombstones of a couple of servants. One is of Robert Scroggie, a footman of the Duchess of Bedford, who once leased the Doune, the house that the Bodach guarded. Nearby is the memorial to Robert Leatham, an English servant to the Marchioness of Abercorn. Both were young men in the prime of life, both moved one of the Homing Stones, and both drowned in the Spey.

The legend says that one of the footmen threw one of the Stones into the river, only for it to return the next day – the Homing Stone came home. It is an interesting story, with the Bodach looking after his own – unless he whistled up the Spey water horse to deal with the interlopers.

NEVER MESS WITH THE CLAVA CAIRNS

The popular Outlander series put Clava Cairns firmly on the tourist map, yet this site is far older than any Jacobite. Clava, not far from Inverness, is a remarkable cemetery from the Bronze Age, so is about 4,000 years old, yet people farmed on the site even earlier. As with Callanish, there is more than one site, with the principal area, Balnuaran of Clava, having three stone circles around burial cairns. But unlike Callanish, the Clava stones have cup-and-ring-marks, decorative symbols with no known meaning. Near to Balnuaran is Milton of Clava, the other site, with a standing stone and a cairn, plus a chapel that dates from the middle ages.

The following wee story is a reminder that, whatever the age of sites like Clava, they still have power. It is best to look, learn and leave, without taking away any stones as a souvenir.

In the year 1999, a tourist from Belgium took a fancy to a loose stone weighing two pounds that he found at Clava. He thought the item looked like a tool from the Stone-Age, so stole it and carried it back to his homeland.

The stone did not appreciate being stolen from Scotland

and retaliated. The Belgian's daughter fell and broke her leg, and then his wife fell ill. Well, such things happen, and the Belgian did not worry unduly, and certainly did not connect his bad luck to the stone he stole from Clava. His ill-fortune continued when he broke his arm, and then, finally, he lost his job.

Wondering what had happened, the Belgian realised that his misfortunes had begun when he stole the stone from Clava. Either unable or unwilling to travel to Scotland, he wrapped the stone in a parcel and sent it to the Inverness Tourist Information Centre. Claiming that the stone was "cursed," the unhappy thief said, "You will probably be laughing at me, but while you are laughing could you please take this stone back to Clava Cairns."

The Tourist Board obliged, returning the stone where it belonged and, hopefully, ending the unfortunate Belgian's run of bad luck. The moral of this story is – don't mess with the Clava Cairns.

CLACH NAM BREATANN

In Scotland, it is very easy to pass stones of surprising historical importance, as few are marked, and many sit on hillsides and among fields. One such is Clach nam Breatann, or Clach Na Briton, in the low hills overlooking Glen Falloch, a few miles north of Loch Lomond and near Crianlarich. Drivers on the A82 pass this stone, or clump of boulders, every day, yet I doubt that one in 10, and possibly fewer than that, understand, or care about, the significance. The name means Stone of the Britons and it is said to mark the boundary between two, or possibly three, of the ancient kingdoms that eventually merged to become Scotland. The British kingdom of Alt Cluid – Strathclyde – was on the south, the Scottish, or Gaelic, kingdom of Dalriada in the north and west, and the Pictish kingdom to the east.

It would be easy to dismiss the stones as unimportant as they appear to be only a mound and a cluster of rocks. However, that would be a massive mistake. The structure may predate the Dark Age kingdoms by some centuries, and the various kings merely utilised the spot as a handy place to have a boundary. The grassy lump may or may not be natural, but the megalith that tops it must surely have been placed there, for what is now an unknown reason.

The kingdoms of Dalriada and Strathclyde often disputed their border. The Annals of Ulster mention one battle fought at a rock known as Minvirc or Minuirc. This battle was said to have taken place in 717 AD, but historians know little more except the Dalriadans were the victors. The Annals of Ulster record is brief:

An encounter between Dál Riata and the Britons at the rock called Minuirc, and the Britons were defeated.

A 19th-century historian named WF Skene first connected the battle at Minuirc with the Clan nan Breatann, and he may well be right, or wrong. It is unfortunate that so much of Scotland's written history was stolen and destroyed by invaders, (I never had much time for Oliver Cromwell, who stole the Scottish records), so the truth may never be known.

Strangely, there is another, similarly named rock, the Clach A Bhreatunnaich which is entirely natural. This boulder rests on the southern slope of Ben Donich and again is said to mark the frontier between Strathclyde and Dalriada. Perhaps both stones survive from a chain of border markers?

CLACKMANNAN

Another stone, better known and better positioned, sits beside the Mercat Cross in the main street in the village of Clackmannan. The very name of the town derives from the stone – Clack from Clach –stone – and Mannan from the person or tribe after whom the stone took its name. And therein lies the strangeness, for who or what was Mannan? We'll come to that in a minute. The visitor's first impression of the stone may well be flawed, for he or she may think it is a fertility item, as it appears like a phallic symbol. Don't be fooled – it is not. The actual stone sits on top of a fairly recent pillar, erected only in 1833 by a man with the eminent name of Robert Bruce of Kennet, together with the minister, Professor Fleming. It is only the topmost rounded lump of rock that concerns us. It is roughly egg-shaped, about three feet long and held together with an iron band. Before its elevation, it had lain on the ground for centuries, beside the town jail and courthouse.

This seemingly ordinary hunk of stone has given its name not only to the town of Clackmannan but also to the surrounding county, which points to some historical importance, even if people have forgotten the original purpose. The name first appeared in the 12th century and has several origin theories. A gentleman named Miller believed it came from "the stone of the monks", which is possible, although why honour that particular stone? In 1926 a man named Watson thought the name derived from the Stone of Manau, presumably from the old kingdom of Manau Goddodin that existed on the southern shores of the Forth. Earlier, in 1888, an academic named John Rhys believed the sea-god Manannan was the origin, which was interesting.

Apart from ancient gods and priests, this chunk of rock has also seen that most splendid of kings, Robert the First, victor of Bannockburn and a dozen other battles and skirmishes. At one time during his campaign to free Scotland from the forces of the English and their allies, King Robert stayed in Clackmannan Tower. When he left, he rested beside the stone, removed his glove and placed it on the stone, as one does.

After he had ridden half a mile, the king discovered he had forgotten his glove. Calling to his servant, he ordered him to return to the clach and fetch his mannan, his glove. The servant replied, "If ye'll just look about ye here, I'll be back wi it directly," and fetched the glove.

Aye, right, as we say.

The town of Clach Mannan is said to have grown around this legend of King Robert's glove, while the place where he stopped is Lookabootye farm. Strangely, one theory is that the stone was originally from Lookabootye Brae, near to the sacred Lady Well.

Mannan or perhaps Mannau is the same sea god from whom the Isle of Man is said to get its name, a pre-Christian Celtic god. If that is correct, then the origin of the stone at

Lookabootye Brae makes sense, for centuries ago, this was a sea loch when the Ice Age receded, and the sea levels were higher than they are now. That would take the history of the stone back thousands of years, predating the Celts, who would take the local tradition and attach their own god to it. I doubt we will ever know the truth about this lump of rock.

GRANNY KEMPOCK'S STONE

I THINK it was Neil Munro's *Para Handy* that first introduced me to Granny Kempock, a figure well known to the people of Gourock on the Firth of Clyde. Granny Kempock, anciently known as the Lang Stane, overlooks Kempock Street, Gourock's shopping street, and stands behind a railing up a flight of steps, marked by a fancy iron gateway. It is a six-foot-high megalith of grey mica schist and the origin is not known, although, as always in Scotland, there are many legends and suggestions.

The name comes from a fanciful resemblance to an old lady, which makes sense, but why is this stone more important than any other in the area? According to legend, it was an altar to some pagan god. Others suggest it marks a forgotten battle site. More recently, people believed the stone brought good luck to two distinct groups.

The first was sailors, who have always been prone to superstition. Before seamen sailed from the Clyde, some would walk around the stone seven times to ensure favourable winds and weather. As well as circling Granny Kempock, mariners and fishermen carried a basketful of sand on their perambulations, while singing, or chanting a song. The words of the song appear to be lost, unfortunately. As the stone is on Kempock Point, it was easily visible from the sea and would be a fine seamark.

The second group were couples about to be married, who needed good fortune even more as they embarked on the perilous seas of matrimony. They also were advised to circle the stone seven times to get Granny Kempock's blessing.

Other, less savoury people also circled the stone. In 1662 a woman named Marie Lamont was one of a group of witches who allegedly danced around the stone during some pagan ceremony. They intended to drop the megalith into the sea and thus sink the ships that passed. Not all witches were innocent old women, then. Some harboured evil intentions.

Granny Kempock's stone has been subject to graffiti over the centuries, with many people carving initials and other symbols. Some may have an as-yet-undiscovered meaning, but most were merely mindless vandalism or people hoping to leave some memory of their lives.

As New Year approached, the people of Gourock would dress up Granny Kempock like the distinguished old lady she is. That sounds like a fine old tradition, and I am sure Auld Granny would appreciate some clothes on a chill night.

MERLIN'S ALTARSTANE, STOBO

Many years ago, in a different life, I was a postman based in Peebles in the Scottish Borders. The postmen were mainly local men, Gutterbluids, as opposed to the incomers, the Stooriefoots, like me, and what they did not know about local legends, history and folklore was not worth knowing.

One delivery route I got to know well was around Stobo, a tiny, straggling village of great antiquity and supreme beauty, with a plethora of history thrown in for good measure. On that route there was the historic Stobo Kirk and a curious stone known as the Altarstone. This stone sits in the wall near the entrance to an abandoned slate quarry and is about two metres in diameter and slightly less than that in height. The nearby farm carries the same name.

According to the few "official" accounts that deign to mention this impressive lump of smooth-surfaced stone, it once formed the altar of a temple. That use seems very unlikely in such a spot. Even less likely was the legend that a witch's claws scratched the exposed south surface of the stone.

However, there is also a legend that Merlin, of King Arthur

fame, was in this area and St Kentigern, otherwise known as St Mungo, converted him to Christianity on the Altarstone. My postman mentor, a gentleman by the name of Archie Kilner, had another story where he related the legend that this is the very stone from where King Arthur pulled the sword that marked him as King of all Britain.

Strangely, the Arthurian connections make sense in the Scottish Borders. The Angles had landed in what is now north-east England and made steady progress against the native British peoples. When they reached what is now the Scottish Borders, their initial progress stopped as British resistance stiffened. Historians know the names of some of the kings of the small British nations that fought back against Anglian invasion. The *Goddodin*, written in the early seventh century, mentions Arthur. That would indicate that Arthur was known to the warriors in this area north of the old Hadrian's Wall and south of the Pictish frontier so he, along with Merlin, was possibly indigenous to what is now Southern Scotland. There are other Arthurian memories in this countryside and further north.

Morgan le Fay was one of history's nasty women, the sort you would not wish to meet on a murky night, or even on a sunny day. She was also the nemesis of Merlin, Arthur's tame wizard, according to some of the legends. It was at Drumelzier, near to the tiny village of Stobo, that Morgan le Fay captured Merlin and trapped him inside a tree, near the Drumelzier, or Powsail, Burn.

A stained glass window in Stobo Kirk also commemorates Merlin. He had already prophesied his triple death, by falling, drowning and being stabbed, and his grave is beside the Powsaill Burn. Naturally, Thomas the Rhymer, the 13th-century Borders knight and prophet, had to get in on the act and stated:

> *"When Tweed and Powsail meet at*
> *Merlin's grave*
> *Scotland and England shall one*
> *monarch have."*

Apparently, this prophecy came true for, when King James VI added the English throne to that of Scotland in 1603, the River Tweed was in flood, and its waters flowed into the Powsail Burn for the first time in recorded history. I would love to see a record of that prophesy that predates 1603!

One legend claims that Guinevere lies buried in the graveyard at Meigle in Perthshire. According to the story, Mordred, King of the Picts, enticed her away or kidnapped her. Arthur led his army north and defeated the Picts, but a Pictish king imprisoned Guinevere at Barry Hill, where there are the remains of an Iron Age hill fort. As she had been unfaithful, Arthur ordered Guinevere torn to pieces by dogs. This story is "proved" by Vanora's Stone in the local churchyard, which shows Guinevere's death, although some people think it really depicts Daniel in the lions' den.

There are other Arthurian place names in the Meigle area, such as Arthurbank and Arthurstone, which was a massive boulder that local people destroyed for building material.

THE STONE OF DESTINY

Sometime in the late 18th or early 19th century, two young ploughmen were walking on Dunsinane in the Sidlaw Hills – the Sidh Law or Fairy Hills – shortly after a very unpleasant winter storm. Heavy rain had encouraged a landslide, which exposed a cave that penetrated deep into the hillside. Getting hold of a lantern, the ploughmen explored the cave, eventually finding a chamber carved out of the rock. As the lantern light revealed more, the ploughmen saw a stairway in one corner of the cavern, with a pile of broken rock blocking access. However, closer to them, dominating the centre of the cavern, sat a large slab of dark stone, with letters carved into it in a strange language. This slab stood on four short pillars or legs.

As they had been hoping for gold or treasure, the two ploughmen withdrew without bothering to check what it was that they had found. It was not until many years later that one of the ploughmen heard the story of the Stone of Destiny.

King Edward Plantagenet of England was determined to add Scotland to his empire, so he invaded with his veteran army. After massacring the civilian population of Berwick upon Tweed, then a Scottish town, Edward defeated the Scottish army at Dunbar and set about raping the country of everything he fancied. One prime target was the Stone of Destiny, where Scottish kings sat at their coronation. Accordingly, Plantagenet raided Scone, where this sacred object remained. The monks at Scone heard that the enemy was coming, so hid the genuine article and hacked out a lump of local sandstone in its place. Plantagenet took the false stone and boasted to all and sundry that he had Scotland's Stone of Destiny.

However, when the ploughmen went to try and recover the real stone, they could not find the cave. To this day, there is speculation about the Stone of Destiny. The one Longshanks stole may be the same as the stone that now resides in Edinburgh Castle, or it may not. The real stone may still be hidden under Dunsinane, waiting for an independent Scotland before it allows somebody to discover it again.

OSSIAN'S STONE

Now, this is a strange one. Ossian was a bard from a couple of thousand years ago, if he existed at all, and he probably lived in Ireland rather than Scotland. Nevertheless, in the Sma' Glen in Perthshire, a boulder has been venerated as Clach Oisein, Ossian's Stone, for centuries. Quite how many centuries, it is hard to say, but the stone is there, and the devotion was undoubtedly genuine.

After the Jacobite rising of 1715, the Irishman, General Wade, was ordered to build a series of roads through the Highlands to facilitate the passage of government troops should another Jacobite rising take place. One of these roads was through Glen Almond.

As the old rhyme states:

> *"If you had seen these roads before they*
> *were made*
> *You would hold up your hands and bless*
> *General Wade."*

The Highlands were generally roadless, impassable for wheeled vehicles except for the Great North Road between Edinburgh and Inverness, and that was not so great either. In 1724, Major-General George Wade became Commander-in-Chief in Scotland, and over the next 15 years, he organised 238 miles of new roads, with soldiers and local Highlanders used for the heavy work.

At the head of what is now called the Sma' Glen, beside the River Almond, and near the road, is a large boulder, seemingly no different from a million others in Highland Scotland. However, this is Clach Oisein, Ossian's Stone. There is no space here to write the full story of Ossian, or of the poet MacPherson who either recounted his tales or fabricated them in the late 18th century. Suffice to say it was a scandal that rocked the literary world and still divides scholars.

Whatever the literary rights or wrongs, in Glen Almond, there was a belief that the ancient bard Ossian lay buried under the stone. When the army was constructing the military road, a huge boulder blocked the projected path. Now the army likes roads, like everything else, to be neat and tidy so, rather than build around the rock, they decided to move it and continue with their straight highway. Although the local population asked them to leave the stone where it was, they continued.

Underneath that stone, the soldiers found a shallow grave, with flat stones surrounding the ashes and bones of a burned human body. While the army was debating what to do with the remains, a group of local men lifted them. The Highlanders carried the bones to a stone circle and, while bagpipes played and the men fired a volley, reburied them in peace. According to a local legend, if people had not appropriately reinterred the bones, disaster would have followed. The last time I was in the Sma' Glen when the wife-woman was bustling to see the gardens at Drummond Castle, the place was as peaceful and beautiful as ever, so the reburial was successful.

CLACH NAN CEANN

On 10 July 2020, my one and only wife suggested we drive to Kinloch Rannoch and points west, an idea that occurred to her due to the easing of the Covid 19 restrictions. Being of a slightly sedentary disposition that month, I resisted her initial enthusiasm but eventually agreed. As most husbands will admit, it is more peaceful to travel than to remain indoors with an unhappy woman.

Herself was right, of course. The wife-woman usually is, although it pains me to admit it. We drove from Dundee through Strathardle to Pitlochry, seeing red squirrels, rabbits and the odd buzzard on the way, then the 20 miles or so to Kinloch Rannoch and onward.

Partway along the southern shore of the loch – that's Loch Rannoch on the old Road to the Isles – we stopped at St Michael's Graveyard, better known as Camghouran, which was the burial ground of the once-local Camerons. These turbulent folk arrived here from Glen Nevis in Lochaber and lived in the traditional way, which means they augmented their farming with cattle reiving and the occasional bout of bloodletting with their old foes of Mackintosh.

As my wife enjoys wandering around graveyards and I like the history of such places, we stopped to look. Just inside the gate of the cemetery, a large stone caught our attention. This stone is Clach Na Ceann, which translates as the Stone of the Heads.

The story behind the name is not pretty, as few tales of clan feud are. The old days in the Highlands were neither romantic nor glorious, but alternated between a struggle for survival against a harsh soil and climate, and pitiless murders between rival clans. Ewan Cameron lived in a house named Tigh na Dige at Camghouran, along with his wife, Marsali MacGregor (another version of the tale claims she was a Duncan rather than a MacGregor). They seemed to live happily, with a gaggle of sons, but there was a rival man on the horizon.

A Mackintosh from Glen Loy had long fancied Marsali. Indeed, he and Ewan Cameron had competed for her, and Marsali had chosen the Cameron over the Mackintosh. After brooding for several years, Mackintosh decided to do something about his long-held desire. Whistling up a band of followers, he led them over the hills to descend on Camghouran, intending to kill Ewan and carry Marsali away with him as his bride.

As luck would have it, Ewan was away on some business of his own, so the Mackintosh asked Marsali where her husband was. When Marsali refused to say, the Mackintosh tried gentle persuasion. He lifted one of her sons and smashed his head against Clach na Ceann, following this up by killing another two of Marsali's sons in the same manner. As the Mackintosh was about to murder a fourth son, Ewan Cameron returned with some Camerons and attacked the Mackintoshes, who promptly ran away.

A bloody pursuit followed, with Ewan Cameron killed in

the skirmishing. The Camerons later raided Glen Moy, but that would be little consolation for Marsali, who buried her husband and three of her sons in the local graveyard, which may have been named St Michaels after the day of the raid, 29 September, St Michael's Day.

Another version of the story says that Mackintosh and Ewan Cameron were both at a market in Perth and Cameron bought a bundle of arrows that Mackintosh also coveted. That slight, added to the jealousy over Marsali, brought on the raid. In this version, up to six of Marsali's sons were brained, but the avenging Camerons killed every Mackintosh except one, who escaped by swimming across the loch. A MacGregor killed him when he arrived. However, Ewan Cameron survived.

Whichever version one chooses, the stone carries a sordid story beside a beautiful loch.

AIREDALE MONUMENT

My final offering to Scotland's stones is also the most modern and undoubtedly one of my favourites. Again, I would not have known about the stone if it had not been for my ever-loving. She suggested that we should go for a walk at East Haven, only a few miles to the north of our home. I demurred, claiming that I had a book to write. So, 10 minutes later, we jumped in the car and drove to East Haven, a tiny little village outside Carnoustie, and a place famed as being a fishing port since at least 1214.

Right at the car park is a massive, 30-ton lump of granite, carved with images of Airedale dogs. Naturally intrigued, I had a wee look, and the information board explained that the monument is to commemorate the part Airedale dogs played in the First World War between 1914 and 1918. The dogs helped wounded men and carried messages in the horrific trenches in France and Flanders. But why commemorate them in this idyllic spot? It seems that Lieutenant Colonel Edwin Richardson trained the dogs here and at Barry Buddon, between Carnoustie and Monifieth.

The Airedale Terrier Club of Scotland raised a massive £50,000 to fund the memorial while local sculptor Bruce Walker carved the superbly evocative images.

L'ENVOI AND A WARNING

The final words here must go to the Brahan Seer, or Coinneach Odhar Fiosaiche, to give him his proper name. Coinneach was born at Baile-na-Cille, in the Island of Lewis in the early 17th century. He lived most of his life in Easter Ross and made many prophesies, some of which seemed impossible at the time, but which have nevertheless come true.

One, in particular, is noteworthy, when Coinneach said:

"Strange as it may seem to you this day, time will come, and it is not far off, when full-rigged ships will be seen sailing eastward and westward by the back of Tomnahurich, near Inverness." This prophecy came true when the Caledonian Canal sliced across Scotland, and ships could sail from Inverness to Fort William.

Another, less cheerful, is said to predict: "The clans will become so effeminate as to flee before an army of sheep." The Highland Clearances proved this correct, as clan chiefs evicted their people by the tens of thousands, preferring the economic benefits of sheep farming to the indigenous people of the land.

Perhaps the most sinister claimed: "The ancient proprietors

of the soil shall give place to strange merchant proprietors, and the whole Highlands will become one huge deer forest; the whole country will be so utterly desolated and depopulated that the crow of a cock shall not be heard north of Druim-Uachdair; the people will emigrate to Islands now unknown, but which shall yet be discovered in the boundless oceans, after which the deer and other wild animals in the huge wilderness shall be exterminated by horrid black rains."

However, Coinneach gave even this forbidding picture a tinge of hope when he added: "The people will then return and take undisturbed possession of the lands of their ancestors."

Much of Coinneach's prophesy rings true today. Year after year, alien people are taking possession of the land of the Gael. Foreign accents from the Middle East, London, Surrey and elsewhere are common. Foreign money is buying out the indigenous people as a wave of non-Gaelic colonists flood into the Highlands and Islands. Many non-Scots own the estates, and non-Scots use the village cottages as holiday homes. Retirees from the south buy up the property, preventing young families from living in the land of their ancestors. This year, 2020, has seen new waves of people escaping the pollution and noise of the southern cities, with more money than the indigenous people can ever earn. The Highlands should be more than just a playground and refuge for wealthy southerners.

Unless some radical action is taken, only the tales will remain, only the ghosts of the Gaels will remain to whisper around cleared clachans. The aliens will have completed the cultural genocide that the Clearances began, and the Highlands will be nothing but an escape and a playground.

Until the day of the horrid black rains.

So there we have it, another slice of strangeness from old Scotland. Every time I select a story, or an anecdote, or a simple fact, I have to dismiss half a dozen more, for this little country

L'ENVOI AND A WARNING

has strangeness under every rock and in every neuk and corrie. I hope you, the reader, enjoyed the stories, so when you walk or drive through the countryside, you can see more depth to the landscape and understand there is more than just scenery in these hills, glens and rain-washed streets.

Jack Strange

Angus, Scotland, September 2020

Dear reader,

We hope you enjoyed reading *More Strange Scotland*. Please take a moment to leave a review, even if it's a short one. Your opinion is important to us.

Discover more books by Jack Strange at https://www.nextchapter.pub/authors/jack-strange-history-humor-united-kingdom

Want to know when one of our books is free or discounted? Join the newsletter at http://eepurl.com/bqqB3H

Best regards,

Jack Strange and the Next Chapter Team

Printed in Dunstable, United Kingdom